Garden with color

Written by
Peggy Brandstrom Pavel
Catherine Rossi

Photography by
William Aplin
Clyde Childress
Michael Landis

Illustrations by Ebet Dudley

Contents

Learning to see and use color

Color influences our every moment, so much so that we usually have very definite ideas about colors. We show them in the clothes we choose to wear and the rooms in which we live. How you color your garden is also a very personal thing. It's only natural to select colors that mean something to you, invoking some special experiences, dreams or memories. If you let your mind drift to garden color, it may reel off images like these:

- ☐ fragile cherry blossoms tossing against a blue sky
- ☐ chrysanthemums and marigolds making a dramatic show of autumn color before the first frost
- ☐ a rambunctious border of sweet alyssum, columbine, snapdragons and larkspur edging a brick wall
- ☐ masses of white wisteria transforming a gazebo into a very private place

Many people assume that planning a garden is like painting a picture on a bare canvas. It is not. Gardeners do not begin with a colorless canvas. Their first step is not to *choose* colors or simply decide upon a scheme of color, but to *see* colors. Your garden is already rich in color if you know where to look. Whether you're perking up an existing flower bed or starting on a bare lot, notice all the tints and shades of color there are to begin with. Even bare earth is not a blank piece of canvas.

Neither is color in the garden permanent, as it is in a painting. Color is constantly changing with the light, the weather, the seasons, maturity cycles of plants, and the people and birds who pass through the garden.

In one way, everyone who witnesses the constantly changing pageant of color in the garden is a color expert. Personal tastes and emotional reactions are as good a guide as any technical rule governing the use of color.

In another way, the true experts are the professionals — the hybridizers, nurserymen, landscape architects and garden designers who analyze and work with color in all its complexities. Experience formulates basic rules, and nurseries and seed catalogs provide the materials.

But look at it a third way, and Mother Nature herself is the top expert in garden color. Not only does she establish

Lavender in the grass is only one unexpected color awaiting the observant gardener.

Colorful floral palettes can be easily achieved by planting masses of flowers side by side.

the basic color schemes and backgrounds, but she breaks her own rules, preposterously, continuously, and breathtakingly.

In this book, we try to bring all three experts together: home gardeners who work with color instinctively, professionals who work knowledgeably, and Mother Nature who works inspiringly.

Any garden designer — whether a landscape architect planning a new garden, or a nurseryman giving advice on which plant for which exposure, or a home owner studying the seed catalogs — is always dealing with color. To the amateur, color may mean only the answer to "What color scheme should I use?" To the professional, the concept of color includes the complexities of depth, texture, hue, tone, proportion, even emotional effect.

The professional knows, for instance, that soft color planted far from the house can make the garden feel larger, and that bright colors planted just outside a window can make a room feel larger. The landscape designer also knows the effects of light and shadow, and is not above manipulating them. A plant with yellow-green foliage, backlit by the sun, has a powerful impact when planted in front of a shaded area of dark greens.

Learn to pay close attention to the shadows of your garden, from far away and from close up. Shadows on grass, on brick, on wet concrete. At the foot of the trees, and under the eaves. On cloudless days at high noon, and on snowy winter evenings at dusk. Shadow color changes constantly with the hour, with the weather, and with the season. And shadows have the power to absorb colors in your garden, subduing everything in their path.

Shade affects growth as much as shadows affect color

Bear in mind, too, that the word "shade" is a part of the word "shadow," and that shade affects growth as much as shadows affect color.

The word "shade" never stands alone in the language of gardening. There is partial shade, half shade, light shade, dappled shade, and deep shade. Shade is a condition that must be carefully considered by the individual gardener. It is one thing where summer days are consistently sunny and bright, and quite another where the garden receives only half the possible sunshine because the sky is often overcast. In the first case, shade is a contrast to be valued, but in the second, shade presents a gloom to be lightened.

As you learn to see shades, you will learn to manipulate them in your garden as you would other colors. Lush ferns, dark ground covers and moss covered rocks have their rightful place when you are trying to spread the coolness of shade, as do colorful bloom or foliage plants when you are trying to counteract its dullness. Learn to observe not only obvious color and light and shade, but all the subtle hues that combine to play in your garden. Armed with the knowledge of what's present, you'll be able to make changes, subtracting and adding to adorn the vast canvas of your garden with eye-pleasing color.

Flowing freeform borders, such as the pink petunias (above), form colorful perimeters around grassy lawns.

An important aspect of gardening with color is selecting proper plants for the light exposure, roses in the sun (left) or impatiens in a shady nook.

The Basic Designer's Colors

Nature has provided us with a rich and varied range of colors as backgrounds on which to begin the coloring of gardens. Often the natural color combination is so visually pleasing that gardeners will opt to stick with the basics, without further color intrusions.

Sometimes our eyes become so accustomed to seeing the familiar colors around us that we forget to consider them as part of the garden scheme. It would seem unnecessary to point out the blues of the sky, the greens of leaves and lawns, or the strong and subtle tones of soil, stone and tree trunks. But take a closer look.

The sky is always there — the whole upper half of the garden picture if you're looking out to the horizon; a leafy-framed umbrella if you're looking up through the treetops. It's seldom the same blue twice. It can be bright and dazzling on a day in early summer; a rich assortment of pastels at sunset; heavy gray just before a storm hits; pale and ghostly when a mist is creeping in; dark velvet at midnight, studded with icy stars.

Lest we forget, green is a garden color, too. Every painter knows it's not a simple color. To discover what a varied palette of hues green actually is, take a short walk through your garden, pretending that you must mix the paint for

The complex color "green" offers countless hues and shades from pale yellowish green to silvery blue-green, and the tones change as they come in and out of shadow. Other basic colors of this garden include bark in white and gray and the background cool gray sky.

Rich tones of the sky at sunset are basic to the garden color scheme.

every green you see: ferns, blades of grass, velvety mosses, and all the foliage from feathery silver to glistening hard greens.

There are countless shades and hues of green in a single lawn. A plant is not the same green when you view it from afar as it is close up. Color, as the human eye perceives it, exists only in the context of what's surrounding it. After all, color is only an illusion of light. The eye mixes the total effect of the hues and shades we view at any given time. Bluish greens in the shadows, yellowish greens in the sunlight, luminous greens with sunlight shining through — it all relates to one color, but there are so many variations that even the classic all-green garden can indeed appear quite colorful.

Rocks and stones come in varying earthy colors, perfect foils for low-growing added color.

Browns and grays are as basic as grass

Browns and grays are as basic to the garden as grass, trees and shrubs, and shouldn't be overlooked as an important part of garden color.

Take another tour of your garden. This time look at tree trunks, branches, and fences. Keep your eyes to the ground and observe pebbles, rocks, gravel and sand. Notice how many color gradations a supposedly colorless area provides — a path, or the house foundation, or a wooden deck.

Watch, too, for the effects of rain or of water from the sprinklers. A cedar fence baked silver by the sun turns a rich, blackish brown when wet, and lightly foliaged plants that normally disappear into the fence stand out suddenly. A redwood deck that weathers slowly from red to brown to gray is transformed back into a dark reddish brown when hosed down before a summer party.

Adding to the Basics

Depending on your viewpoint, Nature has either been extremely benevolent by providing your garden with a pleasing background, or has given you a handicap of serious limitations within which you must work. Successful garden color cooperates with existing backgrounds, be they natural or manmade.

Start with colorful additions that will enhance the hues found in rocks, bark and other natural components of the total garden picture. You may choose to contrast or harmonize and blend as you plant.

Wherever you stand in the garden, you'll probably see a part of a house, garage, fence, or other painted structure, or possibly a natural element with color you'd just as soon not have around. If you were putting the scene on canvas, you could choose to omit an unpleasing or clashing color; you could eliminate it by coming in close; or you could simply change the color, put it in shadow, or paint something else in its place.

As a gardener, however, you cannot eliminate or ignore a structure or a natural element if you don't like its color. Sometimes you may be able to repaint, or you can block the view with greenery, or you can learn to see that a barn-red building, for instance, can be softened and integrated into the garden color plan by planting more of the same or a complementary color around it.

Suppose the offensive structure or natural material is gray stone. You'll discover that pinks and reds look great nearby. Or you may be more inclined to combine yellow tones around gray. If your house is red brick, passionate pink shrubs won't do a thing for it, or for you. But flame azaleas in shades of yellow through apricot will look terrific.

Azaleas in a paler hue echo the rust paint of the barn, softening and integrating the architectural color into the garden scheme.

An earthy background (left) of stone and soil is harmoniously blended with flowers and foliage in soft pastels and creamy white.

The brown bark (above) is a great backdrop for hanging summer color. Early spring color (below) stands out against the browns of the earth and bark.

Color with restraint

Riots of color in the garden are easy to achieve. Just plant according to whim, provide good care, and soon you'll have vivid fiestas bursting into bloom. More difficult to achieve, but usually more satisfying to look at, are gardens where color is kept under control.

High style coloring often calls for planting many different flowers or foliages of one color. The white garden has long been a favorite of professional designers. And what can be more pleasing and soothing than a mixture of white tulips and azaleas, giving way to masses of white lilies, petunias, summer phlox, and finally to a burst of white chrysanthemums before a blanket of white snow? Or you can stay monochromatic by choosing your color, say pink, and laying out the garden plan in shades ranging from the palest blush of pink to rich, deep burgundy.

Using color with restraint doesn't mean just sticking to white or pastels. One way is to choose a dominant color, a subdominant and an accent — for example, by planting mostly bright yellow, some intense orange and just a touch of blue. A basically green garden with bands or borders of brilliant color or a few carefully placed boldly hued accents still keeps the use of obvious color under tight reins.

The white garden (above) remains a designer's favorite, while this pink monochromatic scheme (below) was achieved with container-grown flowers.

Just one bed of vivid red geraniums surrounded with greens is all the color required in the garden on the right.

Hues of the brick patio are repeated in fall foliage and a few containerized flowers in a garden rich with understated color, *opposite*. The white furniture adds brightness.

Color with imagination

Creative gardeners refuse to accept any limitations or preconceived plans imposed on them by the gardening world. Guidelines from garden publications, seed catalogs, nurseries, landscape architects or other professionals cannot halt the inventive mind. When it comes to color, the imaginative gardener is willing to take chances with carefree abandon, to experiment with unusual combinations, to expand conventions of the neighborhood, and to plant the tried and true in exciting new ways.

No matter what technicolor visions your mind can dream up, the world of plants will have something to fit your needs. Pour over the catalogs and our charts (beginning on page 64) to learn ways of expanding your color repertoire.

Chances are that out of every few attempts with inventive color, you'll make a mistake. All is not in vain. Nature is a benevolent shock-absorber of gardening mistakes. If you learn nothing else from this book, we hope you will come to believe what we are constantly relearning: that the garden is forgiving of inexperience. When you make a color mistake in painting a house, buying a car, or decorating a room, you're in trouble; you'll probably have to live for a long while with something you may never learn to like. But when you make a color mistake in the garden, Nature will soon get you off the hook. She softens and incorporates even the wildest colors and the most flamboyant mistakes into her grand scene. What's more, you have the chance to correct your mistakes next season.

Inventive gardeners often team up unexpected garden bedfellows. Orange pyracantha berries (above) espaliered on a stone wall are echoed by orange bougainvillea cascading over the top of the wall.

Santolina repeats the birch bark gray (below) and encloses beds of rust-toned coleus.

Suprising pockets of pink petunias
are interspersed among the juniper
beds that are separated from the
lawn by a brilliant golden band of
dwarf marigolds.

Poppies, violas and alyssum combine
in an unusual border along a
graveled walkway.

Color with mobility

Color in the garden is not a static arrangement. It's a carnival that continuously comes and goes, adding bits of color here and there to keep your eye lively. Often you lose control over the color plan for fleeting periods.

People — working, playing, partying, or lounging — bring things into the garden. Lawn chairs, tables, tablecloths. The everyday tricycle, the Saturday night barbecue, the Monday morning wheelbarrow. An abandoned beach towel, a forgotten sweater, or the laundry billowing on the line. Cushions here and there. Garden gloves, a waiting pot, and the endless summertime hoses, serpentining their bright plastic paths throughout the garden.

Other come-and-go colors are deliberate additions. Quantity and quality of color is easy to control when you garden with container-grown plants or move colorful garden accessories. You can place the color exactly where you want it, for as long as you wish. If the color of a portable plant clashes or becomes unappealing, the "offending" plant can be instantly moved.

Mobile color can call attention to a specific area, designate a picnic spot, lead guests down a path or add cheer to an otherwise bleak period between emerging seasonal flowers. All at a moment's notice.

Think how bleak this deck would be without the transportable garden of impatiens. The total effect and color scheme can easily be changed at a moment's notice simply by moving pots in and out.

A wooden wheelbarrow loaded with chrysanthemums adds a spot of color wherever the mobile gardener wants to park it.

Colorful herbs and lettuce in a terracotta jar add summer color anywhere.

For a bit of summer or autumn brightness in any location around the home or garden, a handcrafted redwood box stuffed with marigolds is easily movable.

Colorful cyclamen attached to bark slabs can be moved about the garden.

Colors for all seasons

Perhaps the success of garden color can only be measured with the passing of the year. Because color in flowers, foliages, berries and vegetables is seasonal, you must learn to plan for the color you want months in advance. The professionals can help you figure out what produces color when. So can our charts starting on page 64.

For most gardeners the headiest time of the year is the annual ritual of rebirth — the march of color from seed and bulb farms to nurseries and garden shops, then to spring gardens everywhere. Through the seasons the garden grows and the color proportions change.

In reality, a garden is like a million paintings, a parade of fleeting visions. Turn a corner and you discover a sudden pool of light. Gaze at the grass through sprinkling water and you catch a flashing rainbow. Try to define or describe or duplicate a color and it disappears while you watch. Leaves fall and huge shadow areas disappear.

It's easy to overlook the gradual day-to-day changes in your garden, but take a second look, in the midst of winter, at a photograph of the summer garden, and you'll know how dramatic and exciting the annual color changes are.

Color is the primary determinant of a garden as art. It is not, however, an art confined to the two dimensions of canvas. It is, wonderfully enough, a living, breathing, everchanging, three-dimensional happening!

Create a joyous work of living garden art by planning for color all year long:

In autumn, nature puts on her most brilliant show of the year.

Spring brings lush green carpeting of grass, vibrant azaleas and flowering fruit trees.

Along a wooden fence, summer annuals are as bright as the season's days.

Silvery crystals overlay dark greens in the winter landscape.

A color wheel from Nature

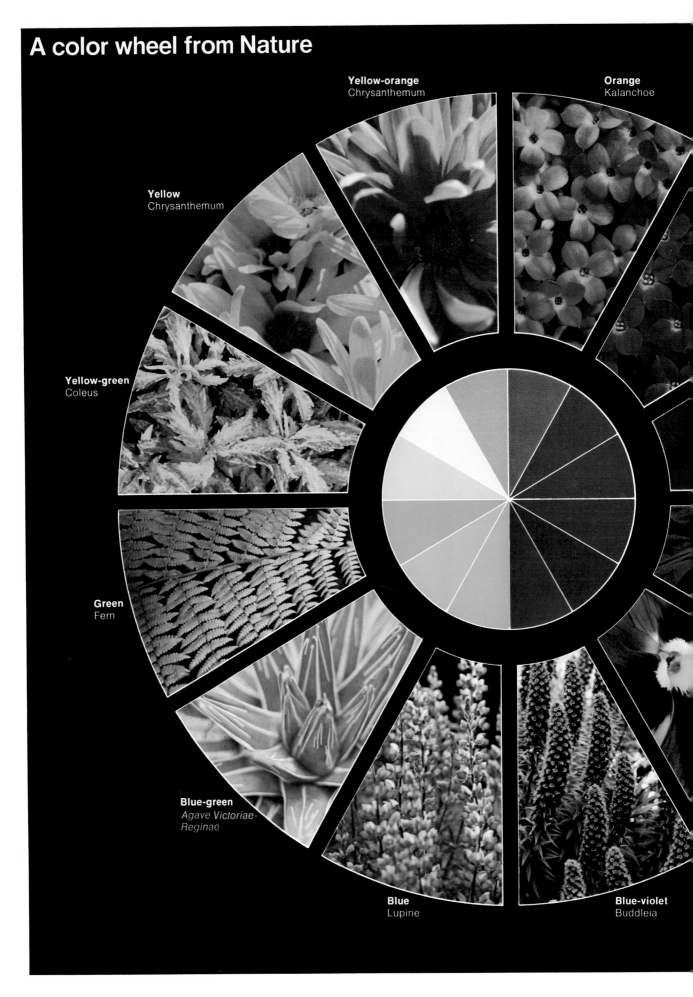

Yellow-orange
Chrysanthemum

Orange
Kalanchoe

Yellow
Chrysanthemum

Yellow-green
Coleus

Green
Fern

Blue-green
*Agave Victoriae-
Reginae*

Blue
Lupine

Blue-violet
Buddleia

Red-orange
Kalanchoe

Red
Poinsettia

Red-violet
Clematis

Violet
Pansy

The principles of color

A color wheel is simply a device that demonstrates color relationships; it begins with the rainbow and shows how colors change as they mix with each other. You already know many of the rudiments of color mixing — you learned them when fingerpainting. Red and yellow make orange. Yellow and blue make green. Blue and red make purple.

The color wheel also indicates which colors contrast to set each other off dramatically, and which blend or harmonize. Blue and yellow, a classic contrast; deepening tones of red towards purple, a classic harmony.

To use this color wheel as an artist would, trace a triangle on a sheet of paper, placing the corners at the three primary colors — red, yellow, and blue. Cut out the triangle; you might wish to paste it to cardboard. As you tilt the triangle, you will find each set of "triad" colors — three colors you can be sure do well together.

Actually, though, a color wheel has limited application to garden planning. For one thing, Nature seldom produces a pure primary color. Very few red flowers, for instance, are as true a red as color wheel red. Most lean towards the blues on one side, or the yellows on the other, or whiten down towards pink.

For another, you are likely to do better without the uniformity of color wheel formulas. Reams have been written on the subject of colors that clash, but no sooner are the rules formulated than someone breaks them beautifully. The greatest offender is Mother Nature herself, who cheerfully combines cerise and green (lunaria), or magenta and orange (lantana), and pleases every beholder.

A better method, if you want a pattern, is to take your color scheme from a flower you particularly admire. (See pages 34-41 for more on this.) But don't shop by color name or label images alone; orange marigolds and orange hibiscus are by no means the same color. Remember, too, that white and gray soften and blend even the brightest colors, so use white blossoms and gray foliage for special effects.

Also, trust your own instincts. A gardener who conscientiously observes the laws of the color wheel will eventually produce a beautiful picture — but so can the gardener who stands back, squints his eyes, and gets stubborn about the exact color he wants for a particular spot.

The following pages take you deeper into our floral color wheel, mostly on the theory that you'll break the rules more bravely and effectively if you are acquainted with the rules.

See colors as artists see them

Here's a brief rundown of the color wheel principles.

Primary colors

Red, yellow, blue. These are the paintbox colors, the three from which all other colors are combined. Whether you use all three together, or any two, or two or three in combination with white, you will produce a show-stopper. They are lively, primitive, demanding.

Secondary colors

Green, violet, orange. Each is a half-and-half mixture of two primary colors. Like the primary colors, combinations of these are dazzling. Because very young children seem to like these colors better than they do primaries, secondary combinations seem unsophisticated, fresh, happy.

Complementary colors

Red with green, yellow with violet, blue with orange — any two colors directly opposite each other on the color wheel. Although contrasts are strong, these combinations are as classic as school colors; in fact, they often *are* school colors. Familiarity and tradition give them dignity, even formality.

Harmonious colors

A spectrum of reds, or yellows, or blues — the colors that merge into each other in the rainbow and are adjacent to each other on the color wheel. Reds into violets, yellows into oranges, blues into purples. Because a combination of such colors varies and builds up a common color, the impact is strong. Remember that a combination of colors that wouldn't work on a pair of argyle socks, or even in a room, can look smashing in the garden.

Intermediate colors

For one sure-fire combination of intermediates you have: yellow-orange, yellow-green, and blue-violet. Each time you move an equilateral triangle one more notch around the color wheel, you will come up with another set. Because you can vary, with each notch, the proportion of primary-to-secondary color, the gradations are endless.

Tints, shades, and tones

Any color mixed with white is a tint. Any color mixed with black is a shade. Any color mixed with black and white (gray) is a tone.

   Mother Nature makes good use of tints, shades, and tones in individual blossoms and leaves, but if a gardener wants to mix tint, shade, or tone, he must rely on the eye of the beholder to do the mixing. There are very few black flowers in nature, but you can add white blooms or gray foliage to other combinations, and sometimes, in certain lights, from certain distances, your own eye will do the mixing.

Primary

Amaranthus

Chrysanthemum

Lupine

Secondary

Complementary

Harmonious

Amaranthus

Fern

Fern

Amaranthus

Tulip

Chrysanthemum

Chrysanthemum

Clematis

Clematis

Fern

Tulip

Lupine

Lupine

Tulip

Clematis

The language of color

We speak of color in many ways. Harsh colors and soft colors. Bold colors and weak colors. Color splashes, and color clashes. Clear colors and muddy colors. Colors that fight, and colors that make peace. Soothing colors and vibrant colors. Loud colors and quiet colors . . . red-letter days, yellow streaks, blue moods, purple rages. Green with envy and in the pink. Most often though, we think in terms of psychological temperature — hot and cold, warm and cool.

These are the warm colors . . .

Red	Red-orange	Orange

Hibiscus

Tulip

Snapdragon

Geranium

Marigold

Ranunculus

Impatiens

Celosia

Marigold

Yellow-orange

Black-eyed Susan

Gazania

Primrose

Primrose

Yellow

Daffodil

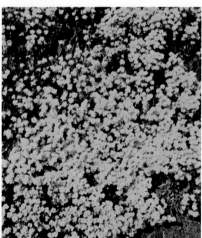

Basket-of-gold

Dahlberg daisy

Yellow-green

Snapdragon

Euphorbia lathyrus

. . . and these are the cool colors

As you see by the foregoing photographs the yellows, oranges, and reds suggest sunshine, flames, and warmth — they almost burn off the page. The greens, blues and violets, on the other hand, feel cool, tranquil, and settled in.

White and gray, too, can be psychological coolers. What says "cool" faster than a crisp green and white planting of baby's-breath? Gray, though, can say either "warm" or "cool," depending upon whether it's the pinky gray of various sedums or the blue-gray of some of the junipers.

Green	Blue-green	Blue

Agapanthus

Agave Victoriae-Reginae

Ageratum

Pachysandra

Japanese flowering kale

Morning-glory

Hyacinth

Sage

Basil

Cineraria

Blue-violet	Violet	Red-violet

Delphinium

Anemone

Crocus

Balloon flower

Canterbury-bells

Verbena

Petunia

Hollyhock

Verbena

Japanese flowering cabbage

Gomphrena

Color is personal

Though an understanding of the color wheel will give you early confidence, it is not necessary for producing brilliantly successful plantings. More important is your own response to color.

You will find no ironclad rules about working with color in this book; a garden is no place for rigidity. But you will do best if you keep a few guiding principles in mind.

The photographs on this page illustrate four basic qualities to look for and work for in your garden. Companion to all of them should be a sharpening sense of scale; outdoor scale is very different from indoor scale, and imposes its own adjustments.

Some people approach colors with the feeling that a few bright spots in the garden make a stronger point than masses of bloom. Some people feel that an honest garden is a grotto of greens, or a cave of earth tones. Some people feel

Contrast. Colors that spark each other bring life and drama.

Compatibility. Colors that blend smoothly suggest peace, depth.

Subtlety. Colors that demand close-ups grow richer by the moment.

Variety. Colors that vary in texture, proportion, mass, seem brighter.

A pocket of alyssum says one thing.   **A river of alyssum says another.**

that since a rainbow doesn't clash, neither can the full spectrum of blossom colors. And some people feel that "less is more" — that color is less a matter of seasonal brilliance than permanent texture.

All approaches can produce beautiful displays. The important thing, if you want to have fun with color, is to trust your own instincts. If a hodgepodge of color says more to you than a disciplined border, plant it. Don't be cowed by fashion, or afraid to experiment. Even failures are eye-filling — and informative as well.

One gardener we know works with color in this way: she thinks in terms of how each plant will function with its neighbors, whether as a quiet foil, or a familiar co-worker, or the center of attraction. With color, as with anything else, all chiefs and no Indians *might* work out well, but you shouldn't really count on it.

There is nothing necessarily dull about an all-green garden.

A small splash of color — these are all primulas — goes a long way.

Color is where you find it

Look at the photograph below. What is the color scheme? If you included the greens and blues and grays of foliage and background, you are already learning to see. You are taking into consideration the subtleties of foliage and background in your color awareness.

In our opening chapter, we discussed ways to see as the professional sees, widening and deepening your color registry. Here we go further, but with some reminders to also see as the child sees, focusing on the small-scale pleasures and surprises that come from close-up scrutiny.

One "exercise" in seeing is to look at each photograph in this book as if it were a jigsaw puzzle. How many piles of different greens would you have to sort out before putting even one tree together? Then look at your own garden in the same way. In just one tree you will find not only endless shades of green, but dozens of other colors, too.

Foliage, bark, fruits and berries, individual blooms — all are miracles in color to an exploring child that are too easily lost in large-scale adulthood. And who looks for color adventure in the vegetable garden? Almost no one, but it's there, waiting to be seen.

Learning to see colors requires a good eye for subtlety as well as for clamor. In this planting, they play nicely against each other.

◁

Pure primary colors aren't limited to flowers. From the vegetable garden: blue 'Ruby Ball' cabbage, red rhubarb chard, and yellow cucumber flower.

Blossoms may be prima donnas of the color garden, but the vivid fall colors of the strawberry plant offer some stiff competition.

Foliage

Blossoms are prima donnas. When they're showing off, it's easy to forget that the real backbone of the garden is foliage.

Most foliage plants are green, but green is a theme with many variations: blue-green, gray-green, yellow-green glossy green, dull green, lively green, quiet green . . . Don't overlook its seasonal mutations; it's one thing in spring, another in summer. And every green is at least two greens at once — the part that's in the sun, and the part that's in the shade.

Nor should you, if you're planning or planting a foliage tapestry, overlook the gray- and red-foliage plants. When you plant a liquidambar or a Chinese pistachio, you plant an annual blaze of fall color. When you plant dusty-miller, you light up your garden at night.

The leaf colors of the various geranium varieties are almost as colorful as the flowers themselves.

1. Lass O'Gorrie	17. Skies of Italy
2. Contrast	18. Mrs. Strong (Double
3. Blazonry	Mrs. Pollock)
4. Distinction	19. Mrs. Henry Cox
5. Display	20. Jubilee (true)
6. Mrs. Burdett Coutts	21. Mrs. Pollock
7. Greetings	22. Mrs. Parker
8. Crystal Palace Gem	23. Attraction
9. Dwarf Gold Leaf	24. Variegated Kleiner
10. Mrs. J. C. Mappin	Liebling (dwarf type)
11. Medallion	25. Variegated Prince
12. Prince Bismarck	Rupert
13. Bronze Beauty	(scented leaf)
14. Marshall MacMahon	26. Flower of Spring
(true)	27. L'Elegante (Mme.
15. Sophia Dumaresque	Margot) (Ivy type)
16. Happy Thought	

**Right:
Like bright Christmas ornaments on a bare tree, persimmons enliven a season that's low on color.**

In this tapestry of foliage colors, dusty-miller edges a border of dark-leaved coleus.

Fruits, berries, and bark

If blossoms are the featured show, and foliage is the background chorus, then fruits and berries are the curtain calls — the color bonuses, the extra gifts.

Seldom as flamboyant as flowers nor as enduring as foliage, fruits and berries nonetheless bring color to the garden the year around. Some of them, like persimmon and pyracantha, show off through fall and winter, just when you need color most.

You'll find many rewards in learning to consider bark in terms of color, too. The bronze and white of birch, the pale tan of eucalyptus, the rust of madrone — all contribute color, form, and texture. And both the silhouette and shadow of a leafless tree can be a rich sculpture in a stark winter garden.

There is a great deal of color in the bark of different trees: the bronze and white of birch . . .

. . . the pale tan of the paper-bark tree.

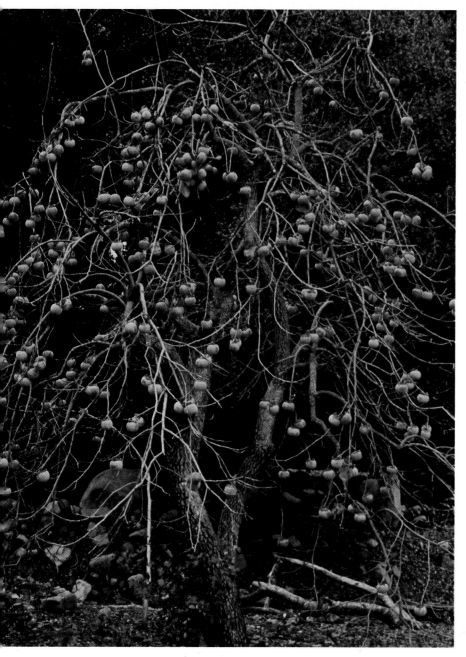

The delicate lavender of eggplant flowers are an added bonus.

Unexpected color

Mother Nature sometimes works in mysterious ways. It's easy to understand that she made flowers in brilliant colors to attract passing butterflies, bees, and other insects for the sake of pollination, and that she even made the few flowers that open only at night a bright white to attract moths.

But it's harder to understand why she chose, so often, to hide some of her richest, subtlest colorworks.

Take the humble bean, for instance, with which she got quite carried away. All the beans in the photograph opposite grow within similar, ordinary looking green pods. In the garden, individually, they are hidden treasure to the appreciative gardener or the curious child; and in a photograph, accumulated, they are a mosaic of color, pattern, and shape.

Perhaps she wanted to show off her own versatility?

Whatever, it's nice to be surprised, and nature is full of surprises. The closer you look, the more you will see. The vegetable garden is a good place to start because color you can eat has a special appeal: the luscious warm glow of a tomato hidden behind dusty foliage; the creamy yellow kernels in perfect rows on a newly husked ear of corn; the delicate and intricate veinings of cabbage, paler towards the center as you peel away each leaf; the miracle of carrots and radishes producing sunshine color underneath the soil . . .

In the food garden, color beckons flirtatiously, but color also *works.* It's a signal to observant gardeners. A pure, vital green indicates a contented, healthy plant. Rich brown soil promises nutrients and good growth. Deepening tones on buds of fruit trees tell the gardener when to spray. And a certain yellowish-green of a summer pear says in no uncertain terms, ''Pick me now.''

Leave an artichoke on the plant past picking time, and you'll never doubt that it's a part of the thistle family.

When you plant a sunflower for the seeds, you get an incredible sunburst in the sky.

Hungarian Yellow Wax peppers are considered an ornamental plant by many gardeners.

The rich red of ripe tomatoes rivals that of any flower.

"Beans, beans . . ." all these beans come from very similar pods, but who would guess that they came in so many shapes, colors, and patterns? *From top to bottom:* Meredith (soy), Richgreen, Giant Green, Charlevoix Dark Red Kidney, Burpee's Stringless Green Pod, Cowpeas, Dixie Speckled Butterpea, Kentucky Wonder, Wade, Wren's Egg Pole, Bountiful, Florida Butter (Speckled Lima), Scarlet Runner, Adzuki, Vermont Cranberry, Oriental Black (soy), Roma, Vermont Cranberry or King's Early, Mung Chinese Salad, Pinto Wyoming #166, Yellow Eye, Altona (soy), Black Valentine, Trout or Jacob's Cattle, Light Red Kidney.

Look into their eyes

Just as it is easy to overlook the subtle or small-scale color effects of foliage, berries, fruits, and bark, it is easy, when you look at a panoramic planting, to miss the galaxy of color each individual blossom provides.

On these eight pages, we present a gallery of close-up flower portraits. As three steps in color appreciation, look into the eyes of these flowers in three different ways: first, as if each were a jigsaw puzzle that you must assemble; second, as if you were a painter and had to reproduce them; and third, as if you were a student and had to deduce color laws from them.

We guarantee that by the third step you will have a profound appreciation for Nature's surprising ways with color. Apparently no one has told her that certain colors do not belong together — like magenta and orange, which she often combines in one flower, or blue and green, which she is forever combining in one plant. The fashion authoritarian who says that cerise clashes with orange has never locked glances with portulaca.

Now go one step further: Take your color scheme for a problem bed from a single beautiful bloom. We show several examples of how well it works.

If Nature can do it, you can, too.

◁

You can duplicate and magnify the pale, delicate pinkish-lavender and faded white of osteospermum in a mass planting of fibrous begonias.

▽

A planting of lilies and sundrops echoes the sunshiny colors of the gazania 'Sunburst.'

The colors of portulaca violate a lot of "rules" but they make a powerful statement when the same combination, with iceplant and nasturtiums, smothers a bank.

The violet and yellow of these crocus can be reproduced on a large scale with yellow and pale violet iris. Red Oriental poppies, like spices in a stew, are optional for sparkle, surprise, self-assertion.

Pink, white, and dark rose gently make friends in the hybrid lily 'Imperial Crimson.' This large-scale planting of chrysanthemums and gomphrena does not duplicate the colors exactly, but the effect is sweetly similar.

One way to duplicate the drama of this parrot tulip's red and yellow is with the unusual combination of nasturtiums and California poppies.

The clean combination of yellow and white in this Iceland poppy appears (right) in an informal planting of Shasta daisies and basket-of-gold.

You can take the red and white of these 'Astro' petunias and recreate the colors in a cool, shady location with red cyclamen and candytuft. Don't forget that green is very much a part of garden color.

Red and yellow is a color combination with many planting possibilities. The red and yellow of the Iceland poppy is equally at home in a border of marigolds and red geraniums. Here, white alyssum lightens the intensity.

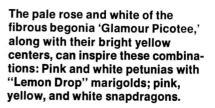

The pale rose and white of the fibrous begonia 'Glamour Picotee,' along with their bright yellow centers, can inspire these combinations: Pink and white petunias with "Lemon Drop" marigolds; pink, yellow, and white snapdragons.

This anemone is another sure-fire color guide. Try a potful of red and white geraniums, or a border of red and white petunias, or a spring display of white stock and red primroses, or, for a fall cutting garden — red asters and white chrysanthemums.

The hot pink and golden yellow of this dahlia suggests pink hollyhocks and tall yellow marigolds, or for fall color, pink and yellow chrysanthemums, or pink bachelor's buttons and dwarf yellow dahlias.

The purity and simplicity of the chrysanthemum "Illini Sparkler" can be duplicated with many annuals and perennials, including white petunias and yellow marigolds, yellow and white primroses, candytuft and yellow violas, Shasta daisies and yellow coreopsis, yellow calendulas and white tulips.

Above left:
For the pure scarlet and pale pink of phlox 'Twinkle,' consider pink petunias and scarlet verbena, or pink and red geraniums, or a mass planting of pink and red dianthus.

Above:
The confetti-like colors of mixed nemesia inspire a freewheeling approach to color combinations.

Below:
The red and yellow of this primrose is classic. To reproduce it, try: 'Red Cascade' petunias and 'First Lady' marigolds, red and yellow zinnias, or red salvia and the yellow basket-of-gold.

Left:
Let this cool delphinium inspire a planting of purple and white violas, or 'Amethyst' verbena and white alyssum, or — if a truer blue and white combination is more to your liking — 'Crystal Palace' lobelia and white petunias, or blue ageratum and 'Carved Ivory' zinnias.

Yellow calendulas, basket-of-gold, and white candytuft were a trial deck planting that was used as a lawn border the following year.

Put it in a pot

Much of the fun of gardening with color comes from experimenting — borrowing a color scheme from a favorite bloom, or inventing your own brave combinations — instead of relying on the tried and true. But it isn't as tempting to experiment on a bed that you must live with all summer as it is with a container that you can hide behind the garage. Smart gardeners use containers for their color explorations.

Pots, tubs, hanging baskets — all offer an opportunity to experiment on a small scale. Would you enjoy living with deep blue and hot pink? Plant cascade petunias in a pot and see. Will you find pale blue and white too weak? Put white and blue violas together and find out. If they pass the test, you can move on to a larger scale in the garden.

Below left:
A small planting of Pacific hybrid primroses will test your tolerance for a strong combination of primary colors.

Golden-yellow, pinkish-orange, and white too wild for a border? Try a pot of nemesia first, and find out.

If you like blue and white 'Perfection' violas in a pot, chances are good that you will like them in the garden.

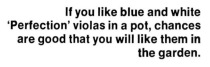

Below:
You can experiment with a "Grandma's garden" — a mixed bouquet of flowers — in a half barrel like this.

If you're not sure whether or not hot pink and purple petunias are for you, gain confidence on a small scale.

If you're shy about color... borrow

A preference for certain colors, or combinations of colors, is often linked to a person's past. In fact, it may be something as simple as never outliving a childhood fascination with the color "popsicle orange."

To deepen your color awareness, we present here 8 pages showing and discussing traditional ways garden colors are used in other parts of the world. As you, an armchair traveler, consider these traditions with borrowing in mind, remember that in real life you will find very few pure "old country" gardens even in the old country. Gardens, by their very nature, welcome transplants and adapt to environment.

With borrowing in mind, consider, too, some of the best gardens of all — the public parks. Neighbors are also a good source of color ideas, whether they're your neighbors or someone else's.

Borrow from the English

Our annual borders are direct descendants of England's cottage gardens — a "sweet disorder" of blossoms of all colors, sizes, and shapes. A rich array of Easter egg colors, all energy is directed into a summer-long display of full garden color.

A sunny perennial border in an English country garden, which its owner described in 1870 as "old fashioned, with no geometric beds but trees, and shrubs, and grass in plenty, and everywhere borders" contained yarrow, Peruvian lily, yellow alyssum, anemones, thrift, snapdragons, columbine, rock cress, campanulas, chrysanthemums, autumn crocus, larkspur, carnations, pinks, gentians, geraniums, baby's-breath, hepaticas, iris, lilies, Maltese-cross, poppies, phlox, cinquefoil, painted daisies, ranunculus, gray-leaved saxifragas, statice, poker plant, and watsonia. The shady borders in this same garden were filled with anemone, arum, cast-iron plant, lilies-of-the-valley, cyclamen, shooting-star, funkia, helebore, daylilies, moneywort, forget-me-not, sundrops, primroses, green-leaved saxifragas, bluebells, spiraea, pansies, sweet violets, and periwinkle.

◁
**A "sweet disorder" of blossoms —
English perennial borders don't rely
on a color scheme, just on the whim
of the gardener.**

Although not on the same scale, this home planting uses a similar color scheme as the one below, and is just as effective.

A mass public planting of tulips employs a simple but effective color scheme of pink, red, and white.

Borrow from the Dutch

It is probably not true that the Dutch are springtime gardeners only, but their way with bulbs is their claim to fame. Masses of tulips, hyacinths, daffodils, and narcissus edge neat brick walks in city gardens as the roses begin to leaf and bud for summer bloom. Low green hedges, carefully manicured, give the narrow gardens unity. Light, bright masses of color, sweet fragrance, and perfect order typify the Dutch garden.

Plant a rich variety of spring bulbs — narcissus, tulips, hyacinth, and daffodils — and there won't be any doubt that spring has arrived.

Borrow from the French

The French love fresh flowers as much as they love good food, and the smallest country dooryard makes room for both. For perfumed profusion plant a potpourri of mignonette and marguerites, lilies and lilacs, violas and primroses. Interplant asparagus and shallots, carrots and lettuce, with nasturtiums and French marigolds. Half a square meter will hold all the herbs you need for a bouquet garni.

Hedge the yard with pink and white hawthorn and edge the door path with anemones, asters, and pinks. It's a very civilized garden, bright with bloom and rich with flavor.

An "old country" spring garden brings calendulas, lettuce, violas, spinach, and other flowers and vegetables together in a small but well-used space.

A planting of parsley, next to the kitchen door, is sparked with the yellow of violas.

Below:
More formal, but still an uninhibited mixture of annuals, herbs, and vegetables.

Borrow from the Italians

Gravel paths, geometric beds edged with brick, and stone garden benches set the scene for the formal Italian garden. Rosemary, lavender, sweet marjoram, and santolina scent the air. Manicured topiaries mark the intersections of the walks, and roses fill the beds. Silver olive trees shade the corners of the garden. It is a sunny, fragrant place for quiet contemplation in the warm afternoon.

A formal herb garden fills the air with special smells of summer — the pride and joy of the gardener and the cook.

The formality of a clipped hedge in a subdued patio sets a quiet, cool mood.

Brick paths, neatly hedged plantings, and seasonal color typify the formal Italian garden.

Borrow from the Spanish

Perhaps the strongest image Americans bring home from the Spanish-speaking countries is the red, green, and white color scheme of crayon-red geraniums and bright green leaves against whitewashed buildings.

But not all is bright and dramatic. The earth tones of terra cotta, clay, adobe, and pebble mosaics are also characteristic of Spanish courtyards.

Earth tones are very much at home in warm-climate gardens, reflecting the colors of the sun.

Even small balconies make room for plants — everywhere the familiar colors of geraniums stand out against whitewashed walls.

Borrow from the Japanese

Tranquility and restraint are the keynotes of the Japanese garden. Although the Japanese greatly appreciate the transitory color of a spring-blooming azalea or a fall-coloring cut-leaf maple, they build their gardens primarily with the enduring colors of evergreens, rocks, bark, moss, lichen, sand. To the uninitiated eye, Japanese gardens seem monochromatic, but there is no better schoolroom for learning to see and appreciate the rich variations of subtle color.

Left: Golden bamboo, a white azalea in bloom, and the grays of rocks and stone, make for a restful scene in this Japanese garden.

Below: Seasonal bursts of color stand out from the subtle colors of the traditional Japanese garden.

Many parks and arboretums have trial plantings of new releases. A good place to see how varieties perform in your area.

Arboretums are a great place to see and learn about color. Most have volunteer groups that benefit interested gardeners.

Borrow from public parks

Traveling Americans probably see more of European parks than they do their own, but in America, too, the tradition of patterned beds persists. While this style of gardening is probably too formal for most home gardens, you can get ideas on color combinations and uses of plants from many park plantings.

Aside from nurseries and garden centers, public parks and arboretums are probably the best places to learn plant names, while you actually see what the plant looks like in a garden situation. If the plants are not labeled or identified in the beds, there is usually someone close by who can answer the question "what kind of plant is that?"

Formal design need not interfere with your appreciation of color. Look for colors and plant forms that you can adapt in your own garden.

How to get garden color

After spending a gray winter thumbing through colorful seed catalogs and gardening magazines, gardeners often find themselves susceptible to a special brand of spring fever. All the common symptoms are present, but for gardeners this yearly "fever" is coupled with: an uncontrollable desire to get their hands in freshly turned, warm earth; the need to walk barefoot across a newly mown lawn, and the desire to witness, once again, the miracle of a sprouting seed.

It's a special time of year — a rejuvenation of spirit, a new day, a chance to start over, an opportunity to try some of the things you only thought about last year. A little advice before you run off: Your first impulse may be to rush to a garden center and buy any plant that satisfies this seasonal urge without thought as to the many conditions the plants will need. You might even buy seeds of anything that looks attractive without first thinking of where it will go, its height, spread, color, and light requirements. Impulse buying can land you in a mess of a garden. Take it easy, curb the enthusiasm a bit, and you'll have plantings to be proud of — and without waste of time and money.

Let's go through a few basics together before you start. We'll help you select a site, prepare the soil, and start many plants from seed. Then we'll plant, feed, and water them and watch them grow and flower before

Our cameras traced the colorful journey of flowering plants from the seed fields to home gardens. In the seed fields, photos, 1, 5, 7, 8; in greenhouses, 13 and 14; in spectacular retail nursery displays, 2, 3, 6, 10. In home gardens, 15 — yellow and blue violas, perennial candy-tuft, with daffodil background; 20 — verbena 'Spirit of '76'; 4 — marigolds 'Nugget mix'; 11 — pink verbena; 12 — variegated impatiens; 9 — geranium 'Cherie'; 16 — Iceland poppies; 17 — impatiens 'Futura'; 18 — nasturtium; 19 — petunias 'Summer Sun'; 21 — zinnias; 22-23 — gazania 'Sunburst.'

your eyes. We won't kid you, there's lots to do and we'll be the first to say that it's not always easy — but we think you'll agree, when it's all over, the pleasure received far outweighs the effort expended. To make the way easier we'll try to show you some mistakes to avoid, some surefire shortcuts to success, and all in all, how to have fun gardening.

The best laid plans...

First, jot your ideas and specific locations on paper. Then, you can visualize the areas in question. Or it's an easy matter to lay the actual areas out with string or the garden hose. This will save you lots of mistakes and digging in the wrong places. Check sun and wind exposures. The charts on pages 64-93 will help you with exposure recommendations.

Probably the most common (and valid) advice we've heard from countless gardeners is: "Don't try to live with an unfavorable soil." Nothing can dampen the enthusiasm of a beginner more than hard-to-manage soil. If your soil has poor drainage (materials to improve it will be discussed later), you might want to consider raised beds, using logs, masonry, or railroad ties.

In your travels, both in printed matter and down the street, keep an open eye for the plant and landscape ideas you like. Spend some time figuring how to adapt them to your own situation. What you see might be a color combination that blends pleasingly with the architecture and other parts of the landscape, or the foliage shape, color, and texture of certain plants that you find particularly pleasing. Take note of the blooming seasons of plants so you can enoy color from early spring to late fall. To help you accomplish this, consult the chart (pages 62-91).

You might want to combine annuals, which are planted each year, with perennials, which come back and flower year after year. You might also

Location For straight rows, let a taut string be your guide . . .

lay down a hose for curves.

For a perfect edge, cut down into the soil first.

Soil

Turn soil thoroughly. Rake off large clumps.

Add conditioners and work into soil.

Homemade compost using the "layer cake" recipe is invaluable in the garden.

Fertilizer Be sure and give new transplants a good start using a dry fertilizer or a liquid concentrate.

want to add some colorful bulbs to lengthen the flowering season. Aim for getting the most out of your space, especially if it's limited.

Location...
look before you leap

Now that your mind is full of ideas, you need to decide where color plantings will look best. We must leave that up to you, but don't forget annuals in pots, tubs, planters, and window boxes, hanging baskets, or even vertical planters. Because of their mobility it's easy to rearrange them as the occasion arises. Use some to brighten a doorway or as a color border to direct traffic to your front door.

Consider spots of color that can be enjoyed from the inside looking out, such as a planting by the kitchen or living room window. Use your color ideas to hide the ugly and accent the beautiful. Camouflage service areas with shrubs accented by colorful annuals and perennials.

Soil ... the basic basic

There are various types of soil, mainly clay or sandy. The ideal soil is one that doesn't readily compact, that drains well but holds enough moisture and nutrients to satisfy the plant. If, when you squeeze a handful of soil and then open your hand, it holds for a few seconds then falls apart, you've got pretty good loam. If it doesn't fall apart, it contains too much clay; if it separates too fast, it's too sandy. You can check with your County Agent if there's doubt about the right type of soil or whether it's the right type for your plants.

Most all soils, clay or sandy, can be improved by amending them with organic matter (peat moss, manure, bark, old sawdust, leaf mold) at the rate of one-third by volume. To explain, let's take a small-scale example. If you dig out, say, nine shovelfuls of soil to make a planting hole, add three shovelfuls of amendment material to the soil pile and mix together before filling in around the plant. If you're going to condition a large area, the quantity of organic matter must be large enough to physically change the structure of the soil. _Enough_ means that at least one-third of the final mix is organic matter.

A compost pile such as the one pictured here is worth its weight in preparing a humusy addition for your flower beds or vegetable garden. You can convert garden waste material to compost in a relatively small area. Moisture, air, and nutrients break the

material down quickly when it's all mixed together. Alternate layers of organic waste material, soil, and add a handful of fertilizer and a handful of lime occasionally. Water it down well and mix it weekly to make it decompose quicker.

Fertilizer...
feeding the hungry

Besides adding conditioners to improve the soil aeration and drainage, you must feed plants to keep them healthy. This can be done with organic or chemical fertilizers. Organic types would include cottonseed meal, blood meal, bone meal, and sludge. They're usually slow reacting, but they don't burn the roots. Follow directions on the package.

There are both dry and liquid chemical fertilizers that are quick acting and safe to use as long as you follow the manufacturer's directions. If you've had a soil test made, the analysis will help you determine which fertilizer to use and how much. If you haven't had your soil tested, a complete, all-purpose fertilizer will satisfy most plants' requirements.

In applying fertilizers — fish, blood meal, commercial liquid or commercial dry fertilizers — follow label directions on the package or bag. Don't try to outguess the manufacturer. Too much of anything, including manure, is dangerous.

The first step in using fertilizer is to understand the label on bags and packages.

There are many formulations but all are listed in three numbers, such as 10-10-10. The numbers represent the percentages of nitrogen, phosphorous, and potassium, in that order. Usually fast-growing, short-season annuals can make it through a complete growing season on one application. However, any check in growth caused by insufficient nutrients can reduce the quality of the plant and its blooms, so it's usually better to make more than one application during the growing season, using smaller amounts, or weaker dilutions. Whenever dry fertilizer is used, follow its application with a good watering. Liquid fertilizer is best applied to a damp (not dry) soil. The need for nitrogen is greater for plants in full sun than for those growing in shade.

Water ... the importance
of a continuous supply

Many plants, such as impatiens, recover remarkably from an occasional oversight in watering, but for best results remember that annuals

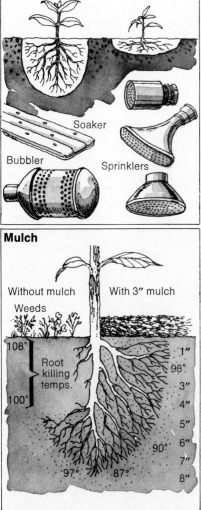

Water
Deep watering promotes deep roots; shallow watering results in shallow roots.

Soaker

Bubbler

Sprinklers

Mulch

Without mulch

With 3" mulch

Weeds

108°
Root killing temps.
100°

1"
98°
3"
4"
5"
90° 6"
7"
97° 87° 8"

need a constant supply to flower and set seed before their year is over. A deep soaking is better than frequent light applications of water. Deep soakings help plants develop deep, strong root systems, able to withstand some neglect. Frequent light waterings result in shallow roots, and encourage diseases and weed growth. A good rule of thumb is: let the soil dry slightly between thorough waterings.

Plants in containers dry out more rapidly than plants in the ground because there is less soil to hold moisture and there is water loss through the sides and bottom of the container. One thing to remember from the beginning is not to fill the containers too full with soil — Leave a space of an inch or so. When soil is too close to the top of a pot or box, you must come back two or three times to really water it. Soak the pot well each time you water — until water runs freely from the drainage hole in the bottom. Double potting (the pot containing the plant is planted in a larger container) requires less frequent watering, and grouping pots together helps to maintain humidity.

Mulching

Mulches conserve moisture, cut down weeding, modify soil temperature, prevent root injury from close cultivation, and improve soil structure and its ability to hold moisture. Obviously, such valuable aids to plants are worth the time, expense, and effort involved in buying and spreading them.

Many different materials can be used for a mulch, including: bark, old sawdust, pebbles, peat or sphagnum moss, leaf mold, pine needles, old manure, compost, rice, almond, or cocoa bean hulls, or even newspapers. Except for plastic and pebbles, mulches have the added advantage of being able to be incorporated into the soil and improving it for the next season.

Apply organic mulches thick enough (3"-4") to prevent weed growth. Some mulches take nitrogen from the soil as they decompose, so additional fertilizer should be added to offset this. Bark and sawdust require an additional ½ pound nitrogen per 50 square feet; rice hulls would need an additional ¼ pound per 50 square feet.

Note: Some of the soil amendments are acid in reaction. Some are neutral. Good gardeners find out the pH of their soil and the amendments they are adding and add lime accordingly. Check with your County Extension Agent.

Whatever mulch you use, pick something that blends well with its surroundings, even though much of this mulch will be hidden by the plants as they grow.

If you don't mulch, then you'll join those who spend a portion of their garden time cultivating and weeding, chores that a mulch normally eliminates. If you do cultivate, keep the hoe close to your toe; shallow cultivation avoids damaging surface roots.

Mulching materials

Material	Remarks
Rotted manure	May contain weed seeds.
Sawdust Wood chips Wood shavings	Low in plant nutrients, decompose slowly, tend to pack down. Well-rotted material preferred. Can be fresh if nitrate of ammonia or nitrate of soda is supplemented at the rate of 1 pound per 100 sq. ft. Keep away from building foundations; may cause termites.
Peat moss	Attractive, available, but expensive for large areas. Should be kept moist at all times.
Ground corn cobs	Excellent for improving soil structure.
Pine needles	Will not mat down. Fairly durable.
Mushroom compost (spent)	This material is often available in areas where commercial mushrooms are produced. It is usually inexpensive, with a good color that blends into the landscape.
Shredded hardwood bark	Makes an excellent mulch that is easy to apply and very attractive. Lasts longer than peat moss, adds valuable organic matter to the soil.
Tree leaves (whole) Tree leaves (shredded)	Excellent source of humus. Rot rapidly, high in nutrients. Oak leaves especially valuable for azaleas, camellias, and rhododendrons.
Hay Grass clippings	Unattractive, but repeated use builds up reserve of available nutrients which lasts for years.
Straw	Same as above, but lower in nutrients although furnishes considerable potassium.
Gravel or stone chips	Limited use, but particularly good for rock garden plantings. Extremely durable, holds down weeds, but does not supply plant nutrients or humus.
Bark	Ground and packaged commercially. Especially attractive in this form. Sometimes available in rough form from pulpwood-loading sites.

Sowing seeds indoors

Growing your own transplants from seed is an important part of gardening. The sprouting of seeds is a bit of a miracle and by starting from scratch, you don't miss any of the sights along the way.

There are certain requirements when starting seeds to achieve a stand of trouble-free seedlings, such as soil, warmth, light (or absence of light), and moisture.

There is a wide range of germinating and growing aids available at nurseries and garden centers. One handy item for the beginner is a seed-starter kit, which contains all the necessary items: soil mix, heating cable, small pots, trays, fertilizer, and labels.

You can purchase pots, flats, peat pellets, soil mix, and all the other accessories separately, and make your own kit, but whatever you decide upon, be sure and keep everything as clean as you can. Use sterile milled sphagnum moss to start seeds in, or use one of the many packaged "soiless" mixes which are disease- and weed-free.

Fill the small flats or pots with the soil mix, wet it thoroughly (warm water helps) and firm it down lightly to form a smooth, even surface. Sow seeds which require no soil covering on the surface of the soil. Sow thinly, tapping the seed out of the packet, or use one of the mechanical seed sowers available, to distribute seeds evenly.

Seeds which do not need to be covered with soil need light to germinate. The light source can be natural sunlight, for as many hours per day as possible, or 24 hours of fluorescent light used at the rate of 20 watts per square foot of lighted area, placed 6 inches from the soil surface.

Some seeds need a covering of soil in order to germinate. A light covering is usually all that's necessary, but check the seed packet for specific depth. Seeds that need a covering of soil do not require light for germination. After sowing seeds, place flats or pots in an area without light, such as a closet. Remove the flats as soon as seeds germinate, and place under lights, or in a spot where they will receive natural sunlight. Remember, all seeds, whether covered or not, must be kept evenly moist through the germination period.

All seeds need some heat in the soil to germinate, but the degree of heat varies with different seeds. The soil temperatures needed for germination of individual varieties are listed for you in the chart in the "Propagation and Culture" column.

Temperature can be provided by heating cables or lights above the seed. When temperatures higher than cables can emit are needed, a piece of clear plastic, formed like a tent around the flat, light and all, will hold in the accumulating heat. The top of a refrigerator or freezer is very warm 24 hours a day, and is an ideal place for flats of seeds covered with plastic. Just be sure to remove the plastic at the first sign of tiny seedlings.

Occasionally, when soil is kept too moist, or temperatures kept too high, soil organisms attack seedlings causing them to fall over. This is called "dampening off." A fungicide applied as a drench to the soil, before and after the tiny seedlings show, will keep this from happening. Lots of air circulation and somewhat cooler temperatures after the seedlings appear, are also good preventive measures.

Now we have the small flats or pots full of soil mix; the seeds have been sown; and tiny green seedlings are showing for the first time. It's time to reduce the temperature (usually 10°-15°) gradually, and cut the lights to 14 hours a day if the seedlings are under 24-hour lighting.

Light placed too far away from the flats or pots results in long, spindly seedlings. High temperatures compound the problem, so keep lights about 8 inches from the tops of the seedlings as they grow.

Another factor which causes spindly growth is crowding, so it's important to transplant the seedlings as soon as they're large enough to handle. Transplant to a 2¼″ peat or plastic pot, or peat pellet. This allows the seedlings more room for root development and gives them a chance to take in more water and nourishment, which results in faster, stronger growth.

If you have space you can eliminate the transplanting procedure by sowing seeds directly to 2¼″ peat pots or pellets. Sow two or more seeds in each, and increase, if you can, the temperature by 10 degrees to offset cooling caused by evaporation. Once the seeds have germinated, snip off all but the strongest seedling, leaving one seedling per pot or pellet.

There are certain seeds which will not germinate under normal conditions. Depending on the variety, the seeds must be either "scarified" or "stratified" before planting.

Scarification is necessary for seeds with unusually hard coats. One way to handle these seeds is to soak them in warm water overnight. In the case of seeds with extremely hard coats you may have to nick, file, or scratch the seed just enough to break through its coat to allow moisture to get in.

Stratification is the subjecting of seed to cold temperatures for a brief period of time to break dormancy within the seed. Usually 6-8 weeks in the bottom of the refrigerator will do. You can sow the seed in its container, and place the container in a plastic bag, or wrap the seed in a piece of moist cotton and put it in a capped jar. Put bag or jar in the refrigerator after the prescribed time. (If scarification or stratification is necessary for the germinating of any seed, it will be noted in the chart.)

Once the small seedlings are growing in individual pots you can place them outside in a cold frame to harden off (acclimate themselves to their new environment). The final step of planting them out in the garden should occur when all danger of frost is over. By then, roots should be coming through the peat pot walls — and garden soil will have warmed up to a safe point.

When transplanting the seedlings into the garden, set the plant about the same depth — perhaps only slightly deeper — than it was growing in the container, to prevent rot.

Problems

You should know that you won't get 100% germination of all seeds planted, but low, or no germination at all, usually results from letting the soil dry out (even once), or soil temperatures that are too low (which you can check with an aquarium thermometer). Often seeds are covered when they shouldn't be, or not when they should be. Too much moisture combined with unfavorable temperatures can rot seed. And, let's face it, once in a while the seed really is at fault.

Leggy seedlings are caused by: lack of sufficient light, too much heat, or not enough food — any stress that denies a plant its optimum growing conditions.

Yellow seedlings are usually the result of root damage caused by too little or too much moisture or fertilizer. Overcrowding of seedlings will also result in yellowing.

A green or whitish fuzz on the soil surface indicates too much water, or lack of sufficient air circulation.

Seed starting accessories

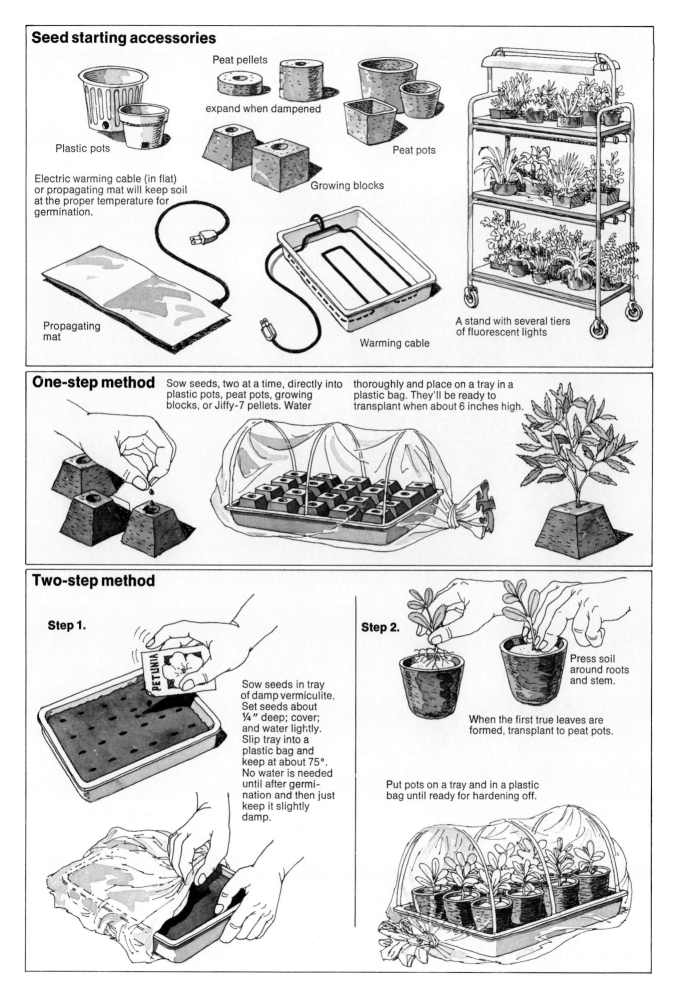

Peat pellets

expand when dampened

Plastic pots

Peat pots

Growing blocks

Electric warming cable (in flat)
or propagating mat will keep soil
at the proper temperature for
germination.

Propagating
mat

Warming cable

A stand with several tiers
of fluorescent lights

One-step method

Sow seeds, two at a time, directly into plastic pots, peat pots, growing blocks, or Jiffy-7 pellets. Water thoroughly and place on a tray in a plastic bag. They'll be ready to transplant when about 6 inches high.

Two-step method

Step 1.

PETUNIA

Sow seeds in tray of damp vermiculite. Set seeds about ¼″ deep; cover; and water lightly. Slip tray into a plastic bag and keep at about 75°. No water is needed until after germination and then just keep it slightly damp.

Step 2.

Press soil around roots and stem.

When the first true leaves are formed, transplant to peat pots.

Put pots on a tray and in a plastic bag until ready for hardening off.

Direct seeding

Fine seeds such as petunia *should* be started indoors. However, other seeds *can* be sown directly outside, in the spot where they are to grow in the garden. This saves messing up the kitchen, but realize that it may give you a smaller percentage of germination because of coarse soil, sun, rain, drying-out, or birds. But don't let that discourage you: If every seed sprouted, you'd have a jungle.

To make outdoor germination easier, fill each planting trench or hole with a small amount of packaged potting soil. This gives you a finer growing medium which holds moisture and usually contains some nutrients. Thin out seedlings when they come up, leaving only the strongest ones.

If you sow fine seeds in rows outdoors, sow them on tissue paper. The seeds show up well, and the paper decomposes rapidly in the soil. Make straight rows with the edge of a board or string stretched between stakes. Use the corner of a hoe blade to dig deep furrows. For shallow furrows, a handle end works well. Always firm the soil over a seed row.

Feed seedlings, whether indoors or out, every other week with a complete fertilizer at one-quarter of the recommended label rate. Increase the strength gradually as the plant grows.

Once you're accustomed to sowing seeds directly outdoors, it is sometimes fun to take all your leftover seeds and donations from gardening friends and mix them all together, scattering them wherever you'd like to see them grow. The results of scatter planting are wild and informal. You can't predict the results, but they're always interesting.

A short cut

Save time and expense by using soil mix only in the row or planting hole where you'll put seeds. Make the seed bed at least 3″ wide and 4″ deep.

Thinning

Thinning seedlings to proper spacing must be done carefully so as not to disturb the roots of plant left behind. Thin with scissors to avoid disturbing roots altogether.

Row planting

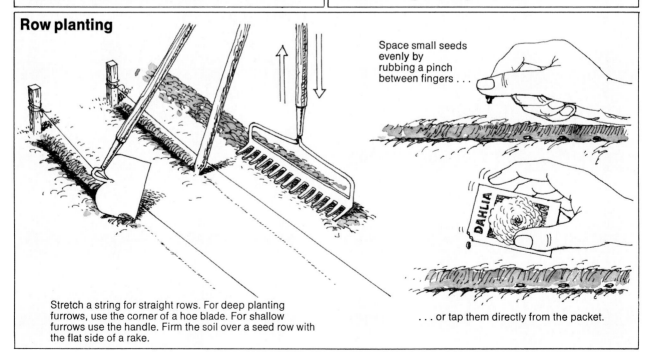

Space small seeds evenly by rubbing a pinch between fingers . . .

. . . or tap them directly from the packet.

Stretch a string for straight rows. For deep planting furrows, use the corner of a hoe blade. For shallow furrows use the handle. Firm the soil over a seed row with the flat side of a rake.

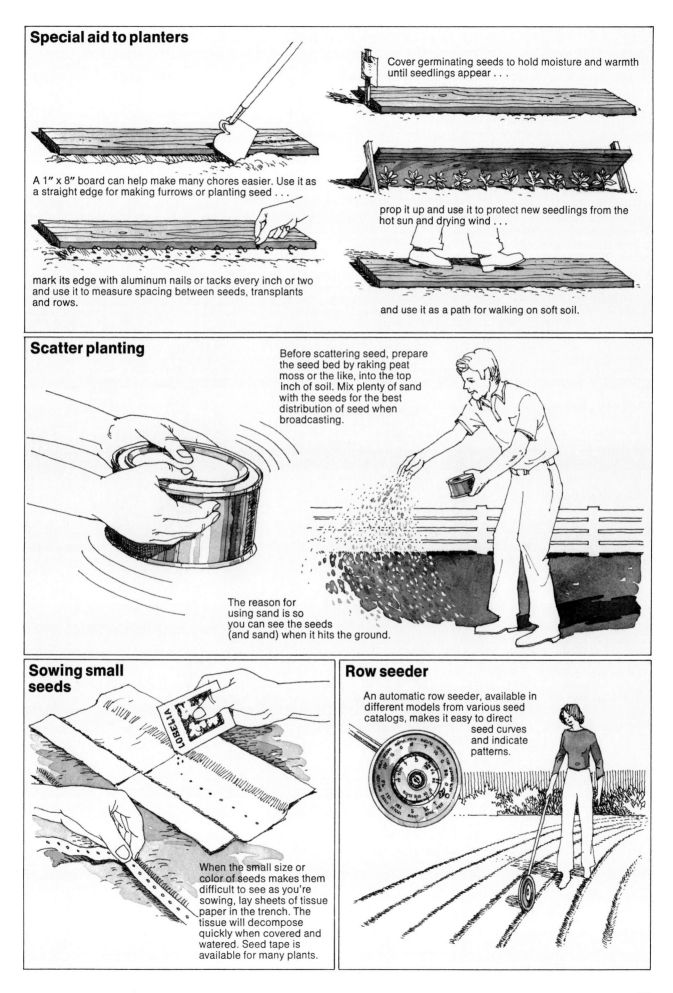

Special aid to planters

Cover germinating seeds to hold moisture and warmth until seedlings appear . . .

A 1" x 8" board can help make many chores easier. Use it as a straight edge for making furrows or planting seed . . .

prop it up and use it to protect new seedlings from the hot sun and drying wind . . .

mark its edge with aluminum nails or tacks every inch or two and use it to measure spacing between seeds, transplants and rows.

and use it as a path for walking on soft soil.

Scatter planting

Before scattering seed, prepare the seed bed by raking peat moss or the like, into the top inch of soil. Mix plenty of sand with the seeds for the best distribution of seed when broadcasting.

The reason for using sand is so you can see the seeds (and sand) when it hits the ground.

Sowing small seeds

LOBELIA

When the small size or color of seeds makes them difficult to see as you're sowing, lay sheets of tissue paper in the trench. The tissue will decompose quickly when covered and watered. Seed tape is available for many plants.

Row seeder

An automatic row seeder, available in different models from various seed catalogs, makes it easy to direct seed curves and indicate patterns.

Transplants

Whenever you transplant seedlings or nursery stock, keep these following points in mind: Prepare and water the planting soil ahead of time; choose nursery stock with compact foliage and good leaf color; and immediately after planting, protect plants from heat, wind, and pests (especially slugs and snails).

It's a temptation, we know, to pick out plants in bloom, but younger plants which have not been pushed to the limit usually give more satisfactory results in the long run. Annuals in bud or sparse bloom are fine, but avoid leggy or heavy-blooming ones.

If you don't get around to planting all the plants in one day, be sure and keep them well watered until you do. They were probably watered every day in the nursery.

Getting them planted

Don't plant dry plants. Water before removing from nursery containers. A damp (not wet) rootball will not fall apart or stick to the edge of the container.

If you plant in the evening or on an overcast day, the plants can get established without stress. If it's hot, set up a simple sunshade of lath or burlap for a day or two.

If you are planting from flats, pull the plants gently apart; don't cut them apart. Don't squeeze the soil or you will compact it and trap roots inside. Plants in packs or containers must be watered and drained before you remove them or the soil may crumble away.

Remove plants the easy way from cell packs and market packs (2 to 12 plants in a flat). Squeeze the bottom of the container in the cell pack to force the rootball above the lip. Snip off any long, coiled, bottom roots and gently scrape side roots with a table knife to direct them outward. Then set plants into their planting holes and firm the soil gently to remove air pockets. Plants should be planted at the same depth as they were in the original container.

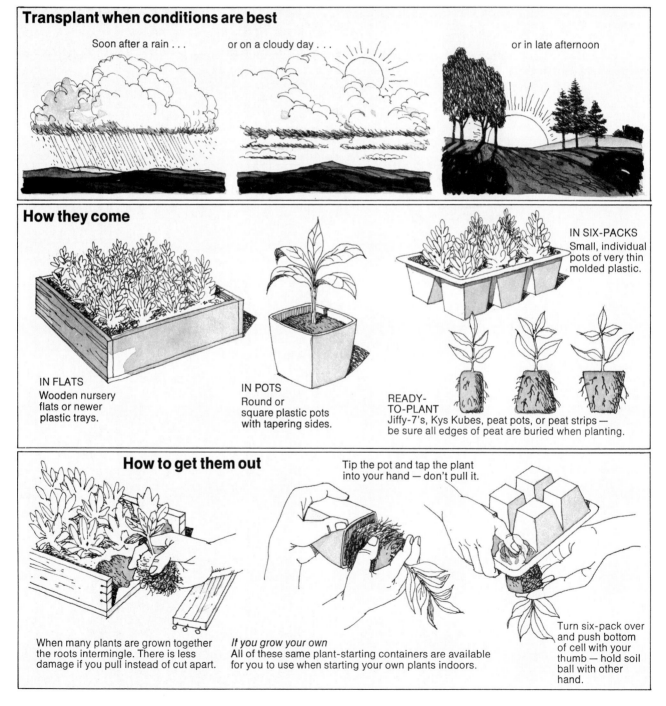

Transplant when conditions are best

Soon after a rain . . . or on a cloudy day . . . or in late afternoon

How they come

IN FLATS
Wooden nursery flats or newer plastic trays.

IN POTS
Round or square plastic pots with tapering sides.

READY-TO-PLANT
Jiffy-7's, Kys Kubes, peat pots, or peat strips — be sure all edges of peat are buried when planting.

IN SIX-PACKS
Small, individual pots of very thin molded plastic.

How to get them out

Tip the pot and tap the plant into your hand — don't pull it.

When many plants are grown together the roots intermingle. There is less damage if you pull instead of cut apart.

If you grow your own
All of these same plant-starting containers are available for you to use when starting your own plants indoors.

Turn six-pack over and push bottom of cell with your thumb — hold soil ball with other hand.

How to plant

Figure carefully how far apart to dig planting holes. Dig holes slightly larger than root ball and water them an hour before planting.

Tear off edges of peat pot to prevent drying and tear bottom to promote root growth. Plant at the same soil level.

When planting seedlings, fill the hole around roots, firm it slightly and water. When water settles, fill again with loose dry soil.

After planting, firm the soil around the root ball and water to remove air pockets and settle the soil. After the soil settles, add enough dry soil mix to fill the hole.

Most all annuals benefit from pinching back, rewarding the gardener with more flowers and bushier plants. Pinch back when plants are about 4″ tall, or immediately after setting out transplants.

Pinching back

A good example of the effects of pinching back. Unpinched plants not only flower less, but have a tendency to fall over.

Annuals have built into them the drive to produce seeds. Their job is done when seeds are formed. Pinch out fading flowers to prevent seed formation and you prolong the blooming period by several weeks. Be sure you get the potential seed pod.

The plants you choose for color

On the following 29 pages we present many candidates for garden color. The list is long, and the charts are filled with information. Here's how to get at it: We've broken the chart into six sections and placed in each one pertinent remarks about the plant.

In the first column ① we list each plant alphabetically by its botanical name, or its common name, whichever is more commonly used.

In the "Life-cycle" column, we show whether it's an annual ② or a perennial ③ . If you run across a biennial, that means the plant flowers the second year from seed, then dies.

Approximate date of bloom ④ may vary somewhat according to weather, variety, and whether it's started indoors.

Numeral ⑤ shows the individual variety or series, and below this ⑥ you'll find the colors it comes in, which will help you to plan your color scheme.

Numeral ⑦ indicates availability from a mail order source, or local nurseries and garden centers. Each source has been given a number:

(1) Ball Company, Box 9055, Sunnyvale, CA 94088. Ball Co. is a wholesale company and does not accept retail mail orders. However, if you cannot find a particular variety in your nursery or garden center for which Ball is a source, drop them a line, and they will give you the address of the nearest retail source.

(2) W. Atlee Burpee Co., 6350 Rutland Avenue, Box 748, Riverside, CA 92502, or Philadelphia, PA 19132, or Clinton, IA 52732 (retail; order catalog from your nearest Burpee branch).

(3) Joseph Harris Co. Inc., Moreton Farm, 3670 Buffalo Rd., Rochester, NY 14624, or Gresham, OR 97030 (retail; order from the nearest branch).

(4) Geo. W. Park Seed Co., Inc., Greenwood, SC 29647 (wholesale-retail).

(5) Stokes Seeds, Inc., Box 548, Buffalo, NY 14240 (retail).

(6) Thompson & Morgan, 401 Kennedy Blvd., Somerdale, NJ 08083 (retail).

(7) de Jager Bulbs, Inc., 188 Asbury St., S. Hamilton, MA 01982 (retail).

(8) Plants available from local nurseries or garden center.

In the fourth column you'll find a description on flower form, foliage, and growing habit ⑧

We've combined propagation and culture as they are natural neighbors. ⑨ shows when to sow indoors; ⑩ whether the seed needs light (do not cover with soil) or absence of light (cover with soil); ⑪ gives the soil temperature for best germination indoors and the number of days it takes to germinate ⑫ ⑬ is the spacing outdoors which, of course, can vary according to the situation. ⑭ recommends the type of soil and drainage and ⑮ the exposure to light or shade. ⑯ in our example gives added recommendations and information. You'll also find in this column what seeds to soak or nick (scarification), along with information on prechilling (stratification) where needed. You'll find which plants to divide, how to make them bloom more and longer, and their weather tolerance.

In the "Use" column ⑰ you will find suggestions on where the plant may be used, either alone or in combinations.

As you look through the charts, you will notice that some plants, those that have many varieties or diverse forms, have been given special charts. They appear above the regular charts, and will help you make a better selection when it comes to planting time.

A final word: If you're looking for a particular plant and you can't find it in the chart, see pages 94, 95. There you will find an alphabetical list of the various other names by which the plant may be known. Directly across from that name you will find its name as it appears in the chart.

Name	Life Cycle: Period of Color	Color	Form	Propagation and Culture	Use
PRIMULA (Primrose)	Annual. Jan.-April. Perennial. Spring-June.	Rhinepearl series: carmine, white, rose, mixed. (1, 4) Laser series: scarlet, yellow, myosotis blue, white, pink, all white with yellow eye. 'Pacific Giants' (3, 7)	Base-branching, flowers borne close to foliage. Rosette with short, strong flower stems.	Seed. Sow annual types indoors June-Sept. Do not cover seed. Keep moist and maintain 70° to germinate in 3-4 weeks. Set out small plants 12" apart in humusy, moist but well-drained soil. Sun to partial shade. Thrives in cool, moist climates. Does not tolerate poor drainage. Sow perennial types indoors in Aug. same as above.	Edging plant for lawn area. Definitely a plant to be used with others, such as candytuft, pansies, calendulas, lettuce, and violas. May be massed in large bed, looks nice edging a wooded path.

Achillea

Achimenes

Agapanthus

Name	Life Cycle: Period of Color	Color	Form	Propagation and Culture	Use
ACHILLEA (Yarrow)	Perennial. Late spring or early summer to early fall.	Yellow: *'Filipendulina'* (4, 6) 'Little Beauty' (4, 6) Rose: 'Rose Beauty' (4) White: 'The Pearl' (2)	Umbel 2' high, bushy. 7" ferny mats. 25" bushy 2' high, dbl.	Seed: Sow indoors in early spring or late fall. Do not cover seed. Keep moist and maintain 70° in soil to germinate in 1-2 weeks. Set out transplants in full sun, 15"-18" apart, in dryish, well-drained soil. Keep moderately moist. Cut back after flowers fade and divide when clumps are crowded.	Plant in herb bed for background color. Use flower spikes for dry arrangements. Try less known rose and white varieties for added color.
ACHIMENES	Perennial. Summer.	Mixed pink, blue, lavender. (4)	6"-12" tubular flowers. Rosette plant.	Seed: Sow indoors covering seed lightly, keeping moist and maintaining 65°-75° in the soil to germinate in 2-3 weeks. Move small plants to pots and keep in partial shade. Rhizomes: Start rhizomes in peat or soil mix, keeping mix barely moist and maintaining 80°-85° in the soil mix until roots and foliage form, then transplant to containers. Keep moist and allow rhizomes to rest 10-12 weeks late fall — early winter before repeating above process.	Pots, planters, or hanging baskets. Store rhizomes after foliage dies. Plant goes dormant until replanted in spring.
AGAPANTHUS (Lily-of-the-Nile)	Perennial. Spring-summer.	Blue, white (8)	Clumps 1'-1½' high. Fragrant flowers on long stems. Evergreen.	Seed: Sow indoors any time. Cover seed lightly. Keep moist and main-tain 75° in the soil to germinate in 3 weeks. Set out 15"-18" apart in full sun or filtered shade and a well-drained soil. Keep moist and divide every 5-6 years. Seeds may be sown outdoors after soil has warmed. Root divisions: Set out in spring as above.	Planter-box subject, with year-round beauty. Plant in clumps or singly in bed. In cold climate grow in containers sunk in ground; lift pots in fall and overwinter indoors.
AGERATUM (Flossflower)	Annual. July to frost.	Blues: 'Blue Mink' (1, 2, 4, 5, 6) 'Blue Angel' (1, 2, 4) 'Royal Blazer' (1, 2, 4, 5) 'Blue Puffs' (2, 4) White: 'Summer Snow' (1, 2, 3, 4, 6) Also pinks, yellows.	Bushy plants 6"-12" with large flowers. Uniform 6" continuous bloomer. 5" 6"-8" short, compact, uniform. 5"	Seed: Sow indoors in Feb.-March. Do not cover seed, keep moist and maintain 70°-75° in soil to germinate in 8 days. Transplant in 4 weeks to 2¼" peat pots, grow cool (60°), set out when roots penetrate pots and weather permits. Seeds may be sown outdoors in May. Sow or set out 8"-12" apart in sun or light shade. Thrives in cool (60°) weather. Keep the rich, well-drained soil moist. In mild-winter areas, plant in late summer for fall color.	Great for mass plant-ings, but try in rock gardens, edgings, borders, boxes, and indoor pots. Try it with other colors to bring out its best. Mix in some whites and pinks with the always popular blues.

Alyssum saxatile

Amaranthus

Allium

Amaryllis

Name	Life Cycle: Period of Color	Color	Form	Propagation and Culture	Use
ALLIUM (Ornamental onion)	Perennial. Summer.	Violet: 'Albopilosum' (2) Rose: 'Ostrowskianum' (6, 7)	Leaves grow 18" long; stem 15" high.	Seed: Sow indoors in spring. Cover seed, keep moist, and maintain 60°-70° in soil to germinate in 3-4 weeks. Set out 6"-8" apart in full sun and a deep, rich, sandy soil. Water moderately. Easy to grow. Bulb: Plant in fall.	A must for the rock garden enthusiast. Delightful as showy edgings. Good cut flower. Showiest in clumps.
ALYSSUM (Aurinia) (Basket-of-gold)	Perennial. Early spring-early May.	'Argenteum' (2) Yellow: 'Gold Dust' (1, 5)	1' bushy. 9"-12" mat.	Seed: Sow indoors in spring. Cover seed, keep moist and maintain 60° in soil to germinate in 3-4 weeks. Set transplants out when soil warms, 10"-12" apart in sun or light shade and in a dryish sandy soil. Self-sows easily. Can also be sown outdoors in May.	Great show for early spring color. Plant in rock garden. Use with candytuft as a charming border, or try some in a stone wall.
AMARANTHUS	Annual. Summer.	Red: 'Early Splendor' (1, 2, 5)	3' bushy flowers in featherlike spikes.	Seed: Sow indoors 6-8 weeks before setting out. Cover lightly. Keep moist and maintain 70°-75° in soil to germinate in 8-10 days. Set out transplants 10"-15" apart in dry, sunny location. Water sparingly.	Summer bedding. Use as background for miniature zinnias or marigolds. Great with wood or stone accents.
AMARYLLIS (Hippeastrum)	Perennial. Spring.	Red, pink, white, salmon (2, 4)	Flowers on 2' stems. Leaves may appear after flowers or with them.	Bulbs: Pot in spring in pots 1" larger than bulb diameter with bulb tip 1" above soil surface. Set in ground 12"-18" apart in early summer. For indoor flowering, lift, repot in Oct. (or when leaves yellow) and rest potted bulb on its side until mid-Nov. Water well, place in low-light area until bud is 6" out of bulb, then bring into brighter light and resume watering and feeding.	Good in containers, or in a single-file row as a spectacular border.
ANCHUSA (Summer forget-me-not)	Perennial. Annual. Summer-fall.	Blue: 'Italica Dropmore' (2, 4) Blue: 'Blue Angel' (2, 6) 'Blue Bird' (2, 6)	Bushy leaves, hairy, 3'-4' high. 9" 18"	Seed: Sow indoors in spring. Cover lightly, keep moist and maintain 70° in soil to germinate in 3-4 weeks. Set out transplants 12"-15" apart in semishade. Trim to keep within bounds.	Use as a bedding plant combined with petunias and marigolds. Use as a filler plant.

Asters

12″
Dwarf Queen

Compact, rounded with a myriad of double flowers. Pots and bedding. Azure-blue, deep blue, crimson, rose, white, mixtures.

12″
Mumsters

More upright than Dwarf Queen with mum-type flowers. Bedding. Red, pink, rose, copper, blue, mixture.

18″
Early Charm

Sturdy. Double flowers. Earliest flowering. Cut flowers. Use for a mass planting of mixed colors.

20″
Massagno

Husky plant wide needle-like petals (spider aster). White, pink, red, scarlet. Good for cutting.

30″
Crego

Most popular, with interlaced petals giving a fluffy effect. For cutting, or as background. Shell-pink, azure-blue, rose-pink, white, dark blue, crimson.

24″-36″
Powder Puffs

Upright plants produce a profusion of double blooms for cutting in one bouquet-type bunch. Pink, azure, crimson, rose, scarlet, white, blue.

30″-36″
Ball Florist Perfection

Large plants with flowers having short, broad, incurving petals that overlap. Azure-blue, peach blossom, pink, purple, rose, white.

Name	Life Cycle: Period of Color	Color	Form	Propagation and Culture	Use
ANEMONE (Windflower)	Perennial. Spring.	Many pinks, reds, violets, whites, blues. (7)	Up to 1½′. Low-growing plants with divided leaves; flowers borne on stalks.	Seed: Sow indoors 6-8 weeks before last spring frost. Cover lightly, keep moist, and maintain 70°-75° in soil to germinate in 15 days. Set out in full sun or light shade in a humus-enriched soil with excellent drainage. Tuberous root. Plant tubers 1″-2″ deep and 8″-12″ apart in Oct.-Nov. Mulch with peat, leafmold.	Combine with narcissus or ranunculus, or grow in containers. In cold areas, plant *A. blanda* (blue, pink, white).
ARABIS (Rock cress)	Perennial. Early spring.	Purple-rose. 'Spring Charm' (4, 5) — Pink. '*Alpina rosea*' (4, 5) — White. 'Snowcap' (2)	Mounding 14″. Quite tender. — 12″ — 6″-10″	Seed: Sow indoors in early spring. Do not cover seed, keep moist and maintain 60° in soil to germinate in 3-4 weeks. Set out transplants 12″-15″ apart in sun and a well-drained soil. Hardy.	Popular for rock gardens and walls. Use like basket-of-gold and perhaps with it.
ARMERIA (Sea pink, thrift)	Perennial. Late spring-early summer.	Pink: Laucheana '*rosea*' (4) 'Formosa' (5)	6″ Dwarf. Narrow leaves form tufts.	Seed: Sow indoors in Feb. First soak seeds 3-4 hours, then cover lightly, keep moist and maintain 70°-75° in soil to germinate in 2-3 weeks. Set out transplants 12″-15″ apart in full sun and a fast-draining soil. Hardy.	Perfect for a dry rock garden. Combine with arabis. Usually planted in clumps.
ASTERS (Callistephus) (China aster)	Annual. Summer-fall.	White, pink, violet, blue, red. (See chart, above.) (1, 2, 3, 4, 5, 6)	1′-3′ high. Many flower forms— quilled, curled, incurved ribbonlike, or interlaced.	Seed: Sow indoors Nov.-Dec. to flower Feb.-April. Cover lightly, keep moist, and maintain 70° in soil to germinate in 8-10 days. Set out transplants 10″-12″ apart in full sun and a good, sandy loam. Thrives in hot, dry conditions. Spray to control insects which transmit aster yellows virus. Destroy infected plants. Change planting locations each year.	Great in cut-flower gardens. Use with zinnias and marigolds, or for added color grow among your vegetables.
BALSAM (Touch-me-not)	Annual. Summer-early fall	Mixture: (1, 2, 3, 4, 5)	2 forms. Dwarf 10″, double flowers. Bushy to 15″.	Seed: Sow indoors in Mar.-Apr. Cover lightly, keep moist, and maintain 75°-80° in soil to germinate in 8 days. Set out 8″-12″ apart in sun and warm, well-drained soil. Does not tolerate wet or cold weather.	Use as background planting with dwarf marigolds or sweet alyssum. Useful border or small hedge.

Fibrous begonia

Let's talk about begonias:

Just about everyone has seen a begonia. Probably it was stuck in a clay pot on a patio and it looked nice; but wait until you really see a begonia. Let it fill a hanging basket or vertical planter. Put it in a window box with ferns or under a tree in a container.

The next time you see one of those ivy topiary animals or figures, imagine it planted with begonias. What a sight that would be, a big white panda bear instead of a green one. You could go on and on and on and . . .

Name	Life Cycle: Period of Color	Color	Form	Propagation and Culture	Use
BEGONIA	Perennial. Treated as an annual. Summer until frost outdoors. Year-round indoors.	Mostly reds, pinks, whites with green or bronze leaves. (1, 2, 3, 4, 5, 6) (See chart, p. 67.)	Dwarf 6"-8". Intermediate 8"-12". Tall12"-24". Fibrous-rooted and tuberous. (See chart, page 67.)	Seed: Sow indoors 16 wks. before setting out. Do not cover the dustlike seed. Keep moist (glass or plastic over flats helps retain moisture and humidity) and maintain 70°-75° in soil to germinate in 2-3 weeks. Use warm water and feed with a standard house plant fertilizer at ¼ strength weekly as seedlings appear. Transplant when large enough to handle to 2¼" peat pots and shift to larger pots or garden when roots emerge from pot walls. Pot up or set out 12"-15" apart in sun or filtered shade and a well-drained, rich soil with humus (peat moss, compost, leafmold) added.	Tubs, pots, baskets, borders, often used with impatiens or ferns. Combine different flowers and leaf colors. Try a vertical garden or a window box with sweet alyssum around the edges. Probably the most versatile color in the garden. Always flowering.
BERGENIA	Perennial. Late spring-early summer.	White, pink, rose. (6)	Large, glossy, evergreen leaves. Flowers on long thick stalks 12"-18".	Seed: Sow indoors in spring or fall. Cover lightly, keep moist and maintain 75° in soil to germinate in 15 days. Set out in partial shade or full sun in cool areas and an average well-drained soil. Cut back yearly to prevent legginess. Watch for slugs and snails.	Good with evergreen shrubs for contrast of color and form — also with red-hot-pokers. Not for coldest areas.
BRACHYCOME (Swan River daisy)	Annual. Late spring to early summer.	Blue, rose, or white cinerarialike flowers. (2, 5, 6)	10" high. Fine, narrow divided leaves.	Seed: Sow outdoors in May where plants are to grow. Cover with ⅛" fine soil in full sun.	Use with poppies, sedum in rock garden or as edging. Plant in masses.
BROWALLIA (Amethyst flower)	Annual. From summer on.	Blue: 'Blue Bells Improved' (1, 2, 4) White: 'Silver Bells' (1, 4, 5) Blue and white: 'Sapphire' (4, 5)	Dwarf, no pinching required. 8" mound. 9"	Seed: Sow indoors in early March. Do not cover, keep moist, and maintain 70° in soil to germinate in 15-20 days. Set transplants, which have been grown at cooler (60°-65°) temperatures, 8"-12" apart or in containers in a loose, well-drained soil. Grow in filtered sun and keep moist. Pinching keeps plants compact. Half-hardy.	Another fascinating basket subject. Use alone or with salmon phlox (annual trailing type). Try it in clay flue tiles set on end.

Fibrous-rooted begonias

Dwarf 6"-8" green-leaved

Derby — White edged with salmon pink. Early. Compact, free-flowering.
Linda — Large-flowered pink. Resists disease and adverse weather. Early.
Red Wonder — Red, compact, free-flowering.
Viva — Snow-white and weather-resistant.
Scarletta — Very popular. Bright scarlet.

Dwarf 6"-8" bronze-leaved

Gin — Rose-pink — very uniform. Free-flowering.
Vodka — Scarlet-red. Weather-resistant. Free-flowering.
Whiskey — White florets held above foliage.
Melody — White edged with salmon-pink.

Intermediate 8"-12" green-leaved

Red Tausendschon — Clear red, small-flowered. Blooms profusely.
Pink Tausendschon — Bright pink. Excellent in pots.
Organdy mixed hybrid — Pink, red, and white.
Glamour series — Large flowers. Early. Pink, red, and rose.

Intermediate 8"-12" bronze-leaved

Othello — Scarlet-orange.
White Comet — White flowers contrast well with dark metallic bronze foliage.
Galaxy — Hybrid in pink, reds, and white.

Tall 12"-14" green-leaved

Fortuna series — Bushy plants with 1½" flowers in rose or bright red.

Tall 12"-18" bronze-leaved

Danica series — Bushy. Large-flowered. Withered flowers do not detract from plant's beauty. Rose and scarlet.

Name	Life Cycle: Period of Color	Color	Form	Propagation and Culture	Use
CALADIUM	Perennial. Grown for colorful leaves, not flowers. Summer.	Various reds, greens, silver, white. (2, 4)	2'-4'	Tuber: Start indoors Feb.-Mar. in peat moss leaving tubers ⅔ exposed, eyes up. Keep *barely* moist until roots and foliage form, then keep moist at all times. Maintain warm 80°-90° temperatures during rooting. Pot up or set out 15"-24" apart (when nights 50° or more) in a humus-enriched, well-drained soil.	Dresses up patio area. Use in tubs alone or with begonias or impatiens. Also, good indoor plant. Great under elephant's-ear (*Culocasia esculenta*) in tubs.
CALCEOLARIA (Pocketbook plant)	Perennial. Grown outdoors as annual. April to fall.	Multicolored, spotted orange, yellow or red.	6"-8" pouch-shaped flowers.	Seed: Sow indoors in Sept. Do not cover seed. Keep moist and maintain 70° in the soil to germinate in 16-18 days. Keep soil slightly moist after germination and pot up or set out transplants 15" apart in semishade and a dry, sandy soil. Water sparingly.	Effective along shaded lawn area or in mass beds near entryway. Adds blotches of color to any otherwise solid green area. Also use indoors.
CALENDULA (Pot marigold)	Annual. Winter-early summer in mild-winter areas. Summer-fall in cool-summer areas.	Yellow, orange: 'Pacific Beauties' (1, 2, 4, 5, 6) 'Kablouna' (4)	15". More resistant to summer heat. 20"	Seed: Sow indoors in Feb.-Mar. for summer bloom, or in Jan. for spring flowering. Cover seed lightly, keep moist, and place flat in total darkness to germinate in 10 days with 70° soil temperature. Pot up or set out 12"-15" apart in full sun in most any soil with good drainage. Performs best in cooler climates.	Probably one of the best bedding plants in cool-climate areas. Plant in fall for color through winter and spring. Great background for pansies and candytuft. Good pot plant.
CALLA LILY (Zantedeschia)	Perennial. Spring.	White, creamy spathes. (2, 4), also gold and pink.	Lance-shaped leaves. Showy spathes.	Seed: Sow indoors, covering lightly, keeping moist, and maintaining 75° in the soil to germinate in 30 days. Pot up or set out in full sun or shade in most types of soil. Keep wet at all times. Rhizomes: Set 4"-6" deep and 12"-24" apart.	A border with lots of character. Looks best on its own. Nice at poolside.
CAMPANULA (Bellflower)	Perennial. (biennial) Spring-summer.	Pink, blue, white: 'Cup-and-Saucer Mixture' (1, 5) 'Fragilis' (4)	3' 6", prostrate.	Seed: Sow indoors in Mar.-Apr. Do not cover seed, keep moist and maintain 70° in the soil to germinate in 15 days. Seed often germinates best when exposed to alternating 3-5 day periods of light and total darkness. Set out transplants in a rich, well-drained soil, 12" apart in sun or partial shade. Very hardy.	Vining types good for hanging-baskets. Grow with white begonias or white sweet alyssum. Use blue lobelia as filler.

Candytuft

Cineraria

Celosia

Name	Life Cycle: Period of Color	Color	Form	Propagation and Culture	Use
CANDYTUFT (Iberis)	Annual. Perennial. Spring.	White: 'Iceberg' (1, 2, 5) 'Fairy mix' (1, 2, 6) White: 'Sempervirens' (1, 2, 3, 4, 6)	Bushy 15" high. 8" extra-dwarf. 9"-12" mat.	Seed: Sow annual types indoors in Nov.-Jan. Cover lightly, keep moist and maintain 70° in the soil to germinate in 8-10 days. Sow perennial types in fall as above except at 65° soil temperatures to germinate in 3 weeks. Perennials flower second season.	Use with primroses, dianthus, pansies, in bright reds, yellows, blues. Looks great as finishing edge of a bed.
CANNA	Perennial. Summer.	White, yellow, orange, pink, and red. (2, 4, 6)	3'-6' high.	Seed: Soak for 24 hours in warm water before sowing indoors in early spring. Cover, keep moist, and maintain 75° in the soil to germinate in 50-60 days. Set plants out 2'-3' apart as soil warms, in full sun and a humus-enriched, well-drained soil. Keep moist during flowering season, remove faded blooms. Tuberous rootstock. Plant as above in spring. Lift and store after first frost blackens tops in colder climates.	Combine with sweet alyssum as ground cover. Good poolside plantings. Plant in tubs or as background feature.
CELOSIA	Annual. Summer-fall.	Many (See chart, page 69.) (1, 2, 3, 4, 5, 6)	2 groups: 'Plumosa' 2½'-3' high 'Cristata' 10"-3' high.	Seed: Sow indoors 6 weeks before planting outdoors. Cover lightly, keep moist and maintain 70° in the soil to germinate in 8-10 days. Note: too early sowing and cold temperatures induce premature flowering, which spoils later performance. Set transplants out 12"-15" apart in sun or light shade and a rich, well-drained soil. Keep moist.	Cristata unique in form. Plant with marigolds or zinnias, in complementary colors. Plant plumosa type with salvia. Flowers dry for winter indoor color.
CERASTIUM (Snow-in-summer)	Perennial. May-June.	White: 'Tomentosum' (2) 'Biebersteinii' (5)	6" creeping mat. 5"	Seed: Sow outdoors, May, at 55°-70°. Germinates in 2-3 weeks. Prefers sunny location, dry soil, but okay in any soil.	Valuable for rock gardens, borders, banks. Plant bright pink dianthus or wallflowers around it.

Celosia

Dwarf 4″-12″ crested

Jewel Box — 4″-5″ extra-dwarf. Yellow, pink, red to purplish red.

Empress Imp — 10″-12″. Red blooms on dwarf plants.

Kardinal Imp. — 10″-12″. Crimson comb. Deep red leaves.

Tall 16″-24″ crested

Floradale — 16″. Scarlet-cerise comb, up to 8″.

Toreador — 18″-20″. Large combs to 12″. Bright red.

Fireglow — 20″-24″. 6″ cardinal-red combs.

Dwarf plume

Feather Mixture — 12″.
Fiery red and bright yellow pyramid-shaped flowers. Branching plants with feathered plumes make attractive container plants.

Semidwarf 18″-24″ plume

Golden Torch — 18″. Golden yellow plumes on bushy green plants.

Crusader — 18″ vivid red plumes on bronze foliage. Dwarf form of Forest Fire.

Red Fox — 24″ carmine-red central plume surrounded by smaller plumes. Bushy.

Tall 30″ plume

Forest Fire — 30″. Brilliant plumes of orange-scarlet. Bronze-red foliage.

Golden Triumph — 30″. Bright yellow plumes on bushy green-leaved plant. Contrasts well with Forest Fire.

Name	Life Cycle: Period of Color	Color	Form	Propagation and Culture	Use
CHEIRANTHUS (Wallflower)	Perennial. Best grown as biennial. Early spring.	Orange: 'Allioni' (4, 5) 'Golden Bedder' (2)	18″ high. 15″ high.	Seed: Sow indoors in summer. Cover lightly, keep moist, and maintain 70°-75° in the soil to germinate in 10 days. From seed to flower in 5 months. Set out transplants 12″-15″ apart in sun and a loose fast-draining soil.	Combine with snap-dragons and dusty-miller. Does best in cool-summer climates.
CHRYSAN-THEMUM	Annual and Perennial. Chrysan-themum Matricaria (Feverfew) Pyrethrum Shasta daisy Late summer-fall.	 Wide range. White and yellow Yellow to red White, yellow center (See chart, page 71.) (1, 2, 3, 4, 5, 6)	 5″-24″ 8″-2′ 3″ 1′-3′ (See chart, page 71.)	Seed: Sow garden types indoors 9 weeks before setting out. Do not cover seed, keep moist, and maintain 70° in the soil to germinate in 15-20 days. Set transplants out when weather permits in sun and a good, humus-enriched soil with excellent drainage. Use shallow cultivation. Space 15″-24″. Sow Shasta daisy type 9 weeks before setting out as above with 60°-70° soil temperatures to germinate in 12 days. Set out as above. Space 15″-18″. Sow pyrethrum types same as above with germination in 2-3 weeks. Culture as above. Sow matricaria types same as above with same culture. Space 12″-15″. Can be grown from cuttings. See page 92.	Good combined with asters or dahlias. Try dwarf types in hanging baskets. Great cut flowers that keep a long time. Plant in pots in spring. Bring indoors in fall when in bloom. Use Shasta daisy with blue delphinium in a mass bed collage.
CINERARIA (Senecio)	Annual. 'Hybridus' Midwinter-April.	Mixes with contrasting eye. Grandiflora: 'Dwarf Giant Ball Exhibition' (1, 4) Multiflora: 'Scarlet' (1, 4)	10″-12″ compact, 10″, small leaves.	Seed: Sow indoors in Aug.-Oct. Do not cover. Keep moist with warm water and maintain 70°-75° in soil to germinate in 10 days. Set out transplants in shade and a cool, moist, rich soil. Not hardy in frost areas.	Excellent in pots. Place in patio or bring indoors for centerpiece. Succeeds outdoors only in mild-winter areas. In cold-winter areas grow in a cool greenhouse.
CLARKIA (Rocky Mountain garland)	Annual. Spring through early summer.	Many pinks, reds, whites. (2, 5, 6)	1′-2′ tall, flowers to 2″ across, leaves long.	Seeds. Sow indoors March. Cover lightly, keep moist, maintain 65°-70° in the soil to germinate in 5 days. Set out transplants in good garden soil and semishade. Does best in cool climates. Sow outdoors in early April. Space 15″ apart.	Use under trees that don't have surface roots or dense foliage.

Coralbells

Coleus

Columbine

Cosmos

Name	Life Cycle: Period of Color	Color	Form	Propagation and Culture	Use
CLEMATIS	Perennial. Summer.	White: *'Henryi'* Blue: 'Prince Phillip' 'Will Goodwin' Red: 'Crimson Star' (2)	All vines to 10' tall.	Seed: Sow indoors after prechilling in refrigerator 6-8 weeks. Cover seed, keep moist, and mantain 70° in soil to germinate in 4-8 weeks. Set out transplants in a rich, loose, fast-draining soil. Set with tops in sun and lower portion in shade, if possible. Mulch roots. Keep moist. Train as a vine on trellis, wall or fence. Cut back varieties that bloom on new wood. Add a handful of lime to each plant in the fall. Work and water the lime in well.	Let it climb a post or fence. Plant begonias around the base to keep roots cool. Fibrous-rooted.
CLEOME (Spider flower)	Annual. From July on.	White: 'Helen Campbell' (1, 2, 4, 5, 6) Pink: 'Rose Queen' (1, 2, 3, 5) 'Pink Queen' (4, 5, 6)	4' high. 3'-4' high. 3'-4' high.	Seed: Sow indoors Mar.-Apr. Often best results are had by prechilling 5 days in refrigerator, then cover seed, keep moist and maintain 70°-80° in the soil to germinate in 10-12 days. Set heat-loving plants in good, well-drained soil and full sun. Keep moist. Weather-resistant.	Excellent hedgelike background plant for petunia bed. Or use at back of vegetable garden.
COLEUS	Annual. Grown for foliage, not flowers.	Many colors. Carefree series (1, 3, 4) Rainbow series (1, 2, 3, 4, 5)	Dwarf, bushy. 8" 18"	Seed: Sow indoors in Feb. Do not cover fine seed. Keep moist and maintain 65°-75° in the soil to germinate in 10-12 days. Set transplants 15"-18" apart in semishade and a moist, humus-enriched soil. Keep flowers removed.	Showy enough by itself in beds or hanging baskets. Keep pinched to maintain bushiness. Edge with sweet alyssum or try it with ferns, impatiens, or begonias.
COLUMBINE (Aquilegia)	Perennial. Spring-early summer.	Many colors. Some popular mixtures. 'Dragonfly' (1, 2) 'McKana' (1, 2, 3, 4, 5) 'Spring Song' (1, 4)	2'-3' high. Flowers usually with long showy spurs.	Seed: Sow indoors in Feb.-March after prechilling 7-10 days in the refrigerator. Cover lightly, keep moist, and maintain 70°-75° in the soil to germinate in 3-4 weeks. Plants may bloom 1st year from seed. Set out transplants 24" apart in sun or semishade, and in a light sandy soil. Keep moist. Hardy, but replace old plants every 3-4 years.	Grow under trees or in beds with anemones. Plant where you can enjoy the interesting flower shapes. Good in arrangements and rock gardens.
CORALBELLS (Heuchera)	Perennial. April-Aug.	Red: 'Splendens' (1, 4, 5) Mixed colors: Red, rose (2, 4, 5, 8)	Ground cover. 2' high. 18" high.	Seed: Sow seed indoors March. Do not cover fine seed. Keep moist and maintain 70° in soil to germinate in 3 weeks. Set out transplants in light shade and humusy soil with good drainage. Keep moist, cultivated, and divide clumps every 3-4 years in fall or spring. To grow from root divisions see page 24.	One of the prettiest border plants to fill in edge of bed. Plant in front of coreopsis, asters, or with begonias.

Chrysanthemum family

Chrysanthemums
Autumn Glory — 5"-6" tall spreading 18"-24" with 1½"-2" semidouble flowers in wide color range. Self-branching. Sept.-Oct.
Korean Sunset — to 24" high. Bushy. Single and double blooms in yellow, gold, pink, crimson, bronze.
Mikado — wide range of colors. Mum, pompon, spider, and anemone types.

Shasta daisy
Little Miss Muffet 12"-15" tall, forms round, compact plants. White flowers with yellow centers. July-August.
Alaska — 24" standard single Shasta daisy. July.
Marconi — to 36" with giant 7" double and semidouble flowers.

Pyrethrum
Robinson's Mixture —
Large 3½" single daisylike flowers on stiff stems. Color mixture includes crimson, pink, and pure white. Vigorous plants to 30" tall. Excellent cut flowers.

Matricaria
(feverfew)
Ball Double White — 24" pure white single and anemone types.
Golden Ball — 8" golden yellow blooms on dwarf, bushy plants.
Snow Ball — 10" pure white with small, double, rounded blooms.
White Stars — 10" white, broad guard petals around button-type center.

Name	Life Cycle: Period of Color	Color	Form	Propagation and Culture	Use
COREOPSIS (Pot-of-gold)	Perennial. Late spring-fall. Annual. Late summer.	Yellows: 'Baby Sun' (4, 5) 'Sunburst' (2) Yellow-orange: 'Tinctoria'	12"-20", compact. 2½' bushy. 2' bushy.	Seed: Sow indoors in early April. Do not cover seed, keep moist, and maintain 70° in the soil to germinate in 21 days. Self-seeds once established. Set out plants 12"-15" apart in full sun. Remove old flowers to prolong bloom.	Plant with marigolds or blue pansies. Excellent summer background color. Good cut flower.
CORNFLOWER (Centaurea) (Bachelor's-button)	Annual. Can be perennial. Late spring-summer.	Blue: 'Blue Boy' (2, 4) 'Jubilee Gem' (1, 2, 5) White: 'Snow Ball' (1, 2, 5) Mixed: 'Polka Dot' (2, 4, 5, 6)	3' high. 15" dwarf, compact. 12" dwarf, mounding. 16" bushy.	Seed: Sow indoors direct in peat pots or pellets in Mar.-April. Cover seeds, keep moist, and place flat in total darkness to germinate at 60°-65° soil temperature in 10 days. Set out in full sun and in a light, neutral soil. Sow seeds outdoors (after all danger of frost has passed) where plants are to grow. Cornflowers do not transplant easily.	Use as background (tall varieties) with dianthus or poppies. Can also dry flowers. Cut flowers fine in arrangements.
COSMOS	Annual. Summer-fall.	Red: 'Dazzler' (2, 5) 'Diablo' (1, 2, 3, 4, 5, 6) Mixed: 'Sensation' (1, 2, 3, 5, 6)	4' 18"-22" 4' Leaves thin, airy, bushy.	Seed: Sow indoors in spring. Cover lightly, keep moist with warm water, and maintain 65°-70° in the soil to germinate in 5 days. Temperatures above 70° inhibit germination. Set transplants in full sun and a sandy, well-drained soil with medium fertility. Drought-resistant and self-sows.	Plant as backdrop for petunias or mini-screen. Dwarf varieties of cornflower would give texture and contrast.
CROCUS	Perennial. Late winter-early spring.	Many. (7)	3"-6" grass-like leaves, cup-shaped flowers.	Set corms 2"-3" deep in light, porous soil in sun or light shade. Mass them for best effect. Divide every 3-4 years.	They give a spring accent. Use in pots, in lawn area, or plant under deciduous trees such as redbud. Bulbs may be forced for indoor blooms.
CUPHEA (Cigar plant)	Perennial grown as annual. Summer-fall.	Red with purple and white. (4, 6)	10"-12" compact mounds.	Seed: Sow indoors in spring without covering seeds. Keep moist and maintain 70° in the soil to germinate in 8 days. Set plants out 6"-10" in sun or partial shade and ordinary soil with lots of moisture. Pinch to induce bushiness. Seeds may also be sown where plants are to grow. To grow from cuttings, see page 92.	Makes an interesting hanging-basket subject. Goes well with trailing type of lobelia. Good border or edging plant.

Dianthus family

**Dianthus
Extra-Dwarf 4″-8″**
Annual:

Wee Willie — 4″ with single flowers in gay blend of colors. Blooms 6-8 weeks from seeding. Spreads 4″.

Charm Series — Husky dwarf, uniform 6″ with 1½″ single, fringed flowers through summer. Coral, crimson, pink, scarlet, white and mixed.

**Dianthus
Dwarf 10″-12″**
Annual:

China Doll — 10″-12″ sturdy, compact with clusters of double flowers in crimson, reds, white, all with markings.

Bravo — 12″ brilliant red, flowering extremely early until late fall.

**Dianthus
Medium 10″-12″**
Annual:

Queen of Hearts — 10″ to 12″ compact plants with brilliant scarlet-red flowers. Bloom begins early and lasts until first frost. Good multi-purpose annual.

**Dianthus
Tall 15″-18″**
Perennial:

Double Mixture — 18″ vivid clusters in combinations of deep reds, pinks, and white, open ringed or spotted.

Makes a brilliant show in early spring. Good candidate for the old-fashioned garden, or for use as a border period.

Name	Life Cycle: Period of Color	Color	Form	Propagation and Culture	Use
CYCLAMEN 	Perennial grown as annual. Early spring.	Tas series Red, salmon, white. (2, 4, 5)	Compact 10″ rosette. Unusual recurved flowers held above foliage.	Seed: Sow indoors Sept.-Nov. Cover lightly, keep moist, and maintain 60° in the soil to germinate in 7-8 weeks. 15 months from seed to flower. Pot up or set out 12″-15″ apart in shaded, ventilated area. Grows best cool (60°-65°) and moderately moist. More easily grown from tubers purchased from nursery.	Pot plant. Protected area like gazebo with ferns or under maple trees. Unusual and long-lasting cut flowers.
DAHLIA 	Annual. Perennial. June to October.	Mixtures of bright colors: 'Early Bird' (1, 2, 6) 'Redskin' (1, 2, 4, 5) 'Rigoletto' (1, 2, 4, 5) 'Cactus Mix' Groups: Decorative Pompon Cactus Others	15″, compact, bushy. 15″, bronze leaves. 24″, one of best. 3′-4′ high.	Seed: Sow indoors in Feb.-Mar. Cover lightly, keep moist and maintain 70°-75° in soil to germinate in 10 days. Transplant when large enough to handle, in 3″ pots. Do not pinch. Set out when weather permits in good, well-drained soil in sun or light shade. Tuberous roots: Plant after all danger of frost 12″ deep, 3-5 feet apart, staking each tuber with the eye pointing toward stake. Cover with 3 inches of soil, filling in hole gradually as plant develops. In cold areas, lift after tops yellow or are blackened by first frost.	Use annual types with lobelia, marigolds, dusty-miller. Plant in containers for portable color. Perennial — combine with mums. Good in a mixed border.
DAISY, ENGLISH (Bellis) 	Perennial grown as biennial. Spring-early summer.	Mixed white, crimson, pink. 'Carpet Mixture' (2, 4) 'Monstrosa' (4, 5) Mixed.	Rosette plant, flowers to 4″ diameter. Doubles.	Seed: Sow indoors in Aug. or Sept. Do not cover, keep moist and maintain 70° in the soil to germinate in 1-2 weeks. Set young plants in sun or partial shade 12″-15″ apart and in a well-drained, humusy soil. Keep moist in summer. This is a cool-weather plant and does not like hot weather.	Use with calendulas or narcissus in spring. Good for border plantings.
DELPHINIUM 	Perennial. Flowers June on.	Pink: 'Astolat' (1, 3, 4, 5) 'Guinevere' (1, 3, 4, 5) White: 'Galahad' (1, 2, 3, 4, 5) Blue: 'Black Knight' (1, 2, 4, 5) 'King Arthur' (1, 2, 3, 4, 5) 'Summer Skies' (1, 3, 4, 5)	5′ high. Flowers borne on large spikes.	Seed: Sow indoors in Jan. Cover lightly, keep moist constantly and maintain 70° in the soil to germinate in 18-20 days. Set out small plants 15″-20″ apart in full sun and a well-drained soil rich in humus. Protect from wind, stake tall plants. Plant parts and seeds are poisonous if eaten. Sow outdoors in August.	Good background planting. Adds a vertical element. Use with nicotiana.

Dianthus family, continued

Carnation
Extra-Dwarf 10″-12″
Annual:
Juliet 10″-12″.
1975 Bronze medal winner.
2½″ fully double, rich
scarlet-red flowers. Sturdy,
base-branching plant. Uniform
habit. Delightful fragrance.

Carnation
Dwarf 12″-14″
Annual:
Fragrance — 12″-14″ dwarf,
compact plants need no
support. Large double flowers
in wide range of colors.
Very fragrant. Stems are stiff
and straight; good for cutting.

Carnation
Medium 14″-16″
Annual:
Enfant de Nice — 14″-16″
stems bear 2½″-3″ fully
double, heavily fringed
flowers. Robust, upright plant
habit. Good for cutting.

Carnation
Tall 18″-20″
Annual:
Chabaud's Giant — 18″-20″,
all colors. large, double,
fringed flowers on strong
stems.
Perennial:
Grenadin — 20″ with extra-
large laciniated flowers on
strong stems. Good cut
flower. "Golden Sun,"
"King of the Black," (darkest
red) pink, red, white, and
mixture.

Name	Life Cycle: Period of Color	Color	Form	Propagation and Culture	Use
DIANTHUS	Annual and perennial. Spring-Summer.	Whites, reds, and variegated. (See chart on preceding page and above.)	3″-2′ high mounds create a low hedge. (See chart, pages 72-73.)	Seed: Sow annual dianthus indoors in March through April. Cover lightly, keep moist constantly, and maintain 70° in the soil to germinate in 7 days. Set transplants in sun and 8″-12″ apart in a light, fast-draining, rich soil. Shear faded blooms. Sow annual carnation types in Feb.-Mar. as above with germination in 2-3 weeks. Culture as above. Sow perennial dianthus in Jan.-Feb. as above, 70°-80° soil temperatures to germinate in 10 days. Culture same as above. Sow perennial carnation types in spring as above at 65°-70° soil temperatures with germination in 2-3 weeks. Culture as above.	Annual dwarfs (Sweet William) dress up any border, plant box, or even a hanging basket. Use taller pinks with snap-dragons or foxglove. Tuck in and around shrubs.
DIGITALIS (Foxglove)	Biennial. May-Sept.	Mixed: 'Excelsior' (1, 2, 3, 4, 5) 'Foxy' (2, 3, 4, 5) White, cream, pink, purple, and yellow.	Vertical growth. 3′ high. 2½′ high. Flowers borne on spikes.	Seed: Sow indoors in spring. Do not cover seed. Keep moist and main-tain 70°-80° in the soil to germinate in 10 days. Set small plants in semi-shade and a rich, moist soil. Watch for snails and slugs. Cut main spike after first flowering to develop side shoots.	Plant petunias at base in bed planting or use in border. Good background plant. Plant against a grape-stake fence. Has an old-fashioned look.
DIMORPHOTHECA (African daisy)	Annual. Summer.	White: 'Glistening White' (1, 4, 6) (black eye, purple edge) Orange: 'Orange Improved' (1) Mixed: 'Aurantiaca' (1, 2, 4, 5)	Spreading habit. 8″ high. 12″ high. 3″ flowers. 3½″ flowers.	Seed: Sow indoors 6-8 weeks before planting out. Cover seed, keep moist, and place in total darkness to germinate in 7 days at 70° soil tem-peratures. Set young plants outside in sun. Will tolerate most soils. Flowers remain open on bright days and close on cloudy days. May also be sown outdoors in May as soil warms.	Great bank cover or ground cover in sunny location. Use with ivy, as ground cover or in a basket.
DUSTY-MILLER (Senecio)	Perennial. Grown for foliage.	Silver foliage: 'Diamond' (1, 2, 4) 'Silverdust' (1, 2, 5)	6″-8″ basal leaves.	Seed: Sow indoors in Feb.-March. Do not cover seeds. Keep moist and maintain 75° in the soil to germinate in 10-15 days. Set young plants in sun and well-drained garden soil. (Check variety for specific germination temperature.)	Woolly gray foliage a must for any garden to show contrast. Grow in front of yellow marigolds. Use to soften color or accent it.

Felicia

Digitalis
Fuchsia
Gazania

Name	Life Cycle: Period of Color	Color	Form	Propagation and Culture	Use
ECHIUM (Viper's bugloss)	Biennial or perennial. Spring.	Usually blue with markings in other colors. Foliage gray-green. (6, 8)	2'-10' Some develop into large shrubs. Unique flower spikes.	Seed: Sow in early spring while soil is still cool, in full sun. Does well in dry, poor soil. Needs good drainage.	Another outstanding rock garden subject. Use with columbine or armeria. Great for seacoast gardens.
ERIGERON (Midsummer aster)	Perennial. Summer.	Lavender: 'Azure Fairy' (4) Pink: 'Pink Jewel' (4)	2½" high, semidouble flowers. 2' high.	Seed: Sow indoors in early spring or late fall. Cover lightly, keep moist, and maintain 65°-70° in the soil to germinate in 2-3 weeks. Set out transplants 8"-12" apart in sun or light shade and a well-drained sandy soil. Moderate watering. Easy to grow.	Plant in the rock garden, border, or for cutting. Plant with snow-in-summer.
ESCHSCHOLZIA (California poppy)	Perennial grown as annual. Spring.	Orange: 'Aurantiaca' (2, 4, 6)	Spreading 1' high.	Seed: Sow early spring or late fall outdoors at 55°. Germinates in 2-3 weeks. Sunny hillside. Prefers cool weather. Readily self-seeds.	Use with rocks in massed natural planting. Good for spring slope planting. Plant lupines to fill in and take over when poppies die back.
EURYOPS	Perennial. Spring to year-round.	Flowers white with yellow centers. Leaves green to gray-green. (8)	3' bush. Leaves finely divided. Tends to get woody.	Buy nursery stock: Sun, little water once established. Keep old blooms picked off. Prune in June.	Background plant between shrubs or next to a wall. Another super seacoast plant.
FELICIA (Blue marguerite)	Perennial. Spring-summer.	Sky-blue flowers, yellow eyes, daisylike: 'San Gabriel' 'Santa Anita' (4, 8)	1½' high, spreading 4'-5'.	Seed: Sow indoors anytime. Cover lightly, keep moist, and maintain 75° in the soil to germinate in 2 weeks. Set out in sunny spot. Prune back in late summer and pick off dead blooms.	Bedding plant. Use with marigolds or zinnias in raised wooden beds or plant in ground against outdoor bench or gazebo. Makes a good specimen.

Let's talk about geraniums

Few plants provide more lasting pleasure in the garden. There are colors and growth habits to suit all tastes. Whatever use you may want of a plant, one type of geranium or another will fill it — shrubs for the border or containers on a sunny patio; vines for hanging baskets or quick ground cover. They take little care, bloom their heads off, and are great for cut flowers.

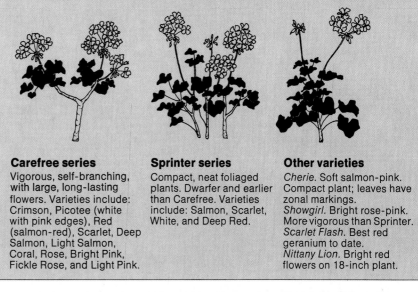

Geraniums

Geranium varieties which grow true from seed are a relatively recent introduction. Approximate number of weeks from seed to flower varies from 15 to 20 weeks.

Carefree series
Vigorous, self-branching, with large, long-lasting flowers. Varieties include: Crimson, Picotee (white with pink edges), Red (salmon-red), Scarlet, Deep Salmon, Light Salmon, Coral, Rose, Bright Pink, Fickle Rose, and Light Pink.

Sprinter series
Compact, neat foliaged plants. Dwarfer and earlier than Carefree. Varieties include: Salmon, Scarlet, White, and Deep Red.

Other varieties
Cherie. Soft salmon-pink. Compact plant; leaves have zonal markings. *Showgirl.* Bright rose-pink. More vigorous than Sprinter. *Scarlet Flash.* Best red geranium to date. *Nittany Lion.* Bright red flowers on 18-inch plant.

Name	Life Cycle: Period of Color	Color	Form	Propagation and Culture	Use
FORGET-ME-NOT (Myosotis)	Biennial. Spring.	Blue: 'Blue Bird' (1, 2, 4) 'Victorla' (3, 5) 'Ultramarine'	5"-8" dwarf, compact.	Seed: Sow indoors Dec.-Jan. Cover seed, keep moist, place flat in total darkness and maintain 65°-75° in the soil to germinate in 2-3 weeks. Set out small plants in partial shade and a well-drained soil.	Excellent carpet under tulips and daffodils. Pretty with pansies.
FREESIA	Perennial. Early spring.	Many colors, varieties: white, violet, pink, yellow, blue, orange. (seed: 4, 5; corms: 7)	Basal grass-like leaves. Grows up to 18".	Corms: 2" deep with pointed ends up in a sunny location and well-drained soil in the fall. Freesias may be forced for early flowering in pots. Seed: Sow July-Aug. Often blooms following spring.	Plant under trees or large shrubs in mild-winter areas. Grow in pots in cold-winter areas.
FUCHSIA (Lady's-ear-drops)	Tender perennial. Ever-blooming in mild climates.	Many bicolors with red, pink, lavender. Also single colors and white. (6, 8)	Erect and trailing.	Seed: Sow indoors in January on surface of soil mix. Do not cover seed. Keep moist. Maintain 70°-75° in soil to germinate in 2-6 weeks. Transplant when large enough to handle to 2¼" peat pots and grow on at cool (60°) temperatures. Shift to 4" pots or to final location when roots emerge. Prefers cool summer and modified sunlight. Prune in spring.	Beautful hanging-basket subject. Use with impatiens or begonias. Upright forms are excellent in tubs.
GAILLARDIA (Blanket flower)	Annual. Perennial. Spring, summer to frost.	Various yellows, oranges, mixed: 'Lollipop' series (2, 3, 4) 'Monarch' strain: (1, 4, 5)	10" mound. 2' high.	Seed: Sow indoors in March at 70° soil temperature. Light is needed so do not cover seed. Germinates in 2-3 weeks. Set out transplants after soil has warmed 12"-15" apart in full sun and well-drained, humusy soil. Thrives in heat. Remove faded flowers for continuous blooms.	Use with calendula, Iceland poppies, and maltese-cross.
GAZANIA	Perennial in warm climates; annual elsewhere. Spring-summer.	Mixed colors (red, orange, yellow) with contrasting eye. 'Sunshine' (1, 2, 3, 4, 6)	6"-8" plant. Ground cover.	Seed: Sow indoors Feb.-Mar. Cover seed. Keep moist and maintain 60° in soil to germinate in 10 days. Thrives on heat so set out transplants 12"-15" apart in full sun and somewhat dry soil. Some flowers close at night.	Edging for lawn area. Pot plant; use with celosia, lobelia, sweet alyssum. Good for hanging baskets. Unique color patterns inside each individual flower.

Gomphrena

Impatiens

Let's talk about impatiens

When you think of impatiens think of colorful, bright stars twinkling against a green or greenish-white background. Although they look magnificent in hanging baskets, plant some in raised beds, vertical wall planters, or as a shaded ground cover. They like shade but will take the sun as long as they are watered generously. Mix them with other plants or let them stand on their own. Whatever you do, they will bring much enjoyment to any gardener.

Name	Life Cycle: Period of Color	Color	Form	Propagation and Culture	Use
GERANIUM (Pelargonium)	Perennial grown as annual.	Red, pink, white (See chart, page 75.) (1, 2, 3, 4, 5, 6)	Various (See chart, page 75.)	Seed: Sow indoors 10-12 weeks before setting out. Cover seed ⅛", keep moist and maintain a minimum 75° in soil during the 2-4 week germination period. Set out plants 18"-24" apart in full sun or light shade in good, well-drained soil. Keep moderately moist and remove faded blooms to encourage continuous flowering.	Good in pots or massed in beds. Red varieties very showy. Geraniums are true perennials in mild-climate regions.
GERBERA (Transvaal daisy)	Perennial. Early summer-late fall.	Red, orange, yellow, singles and doubles. (2, 4, 5)	Clumps with long flowering stems.	Seed: Sow indoors Jan.-Feb. Cover seed lightly. Keep moist and maintain 70°-75° in soil to germinate in 10 days. From seed to flower: 12-18 months. Set out transplants 12"-15" apart in full sun to partial shade and good humusy soil with excellent drainage. Withstands heat. Protect from snails and slugs.	Good background for impatiens. Excellent cut flowers. For warm climates. Grow in pots where ground freezes.
GEUM (Rose-of-the-rockery)	Perennial. Summer.	Yellow: 'Lady Stratheden' (2, 4, 5) Scarlet: 'Mrs. Bradshaw' (2, 4, 5)	Tall, slender. 2' high. 2' high.	Seed: Sow indoors Feb. Cover seed lightly, keep moist, and maintain 70° in soil to germinate in 3-4 weeks. Seed may be sown outdoors in May. Set out transplants 12"-15" apart in full sun or partial shade in well-drained or ordinary soil. Remove faded blooms.	Colorful single subject or as a border. Good in rock gardens.
GLADIOLUS	Perennial. Spring-fall.	Wide range: white, pink, red, lilac, yellow. (2, 4)	Up to 5'.	Corms: Plant 2"-4" apart and 4 times their thickness in garden when soil warms in spring. Set out in good, well-drained soil in full sun. Plant every two weeks for succession of blooms.	Use as a border with delphinium, Shasta daisy, phlox, iris.
GLOXINIA (Sinningia)	Perennial.	Blue, purple, pink, red, white. (2, 4)	Large rosette of oblong leaves, bell-shaped flowers.	Seed: Sow indoors anytime on surface of soil mix. Do not cover seed. Keep moist and maintain 70°-75° in soil. Tubers: Plant 1" deep Dec.-March. Water sparingly until leaves appear. Maintain 70°-75°. Feed established plants regularly. Keep water off foliage, reducing water after flowering to store tuber in cool, dark place. Keep plants in shaded area.	Pot subject on shaded patio or indoors in sunny window — but not full, direct sun.

Impatiens

Dwarf 6″-10″

Elfin — 1″-1½″ flowers, space 12″-15″. Do not pinch (self-branching), very compact. Flowers early summer until frost. Use in beds, tubs, boxes, or hanging baskets.

Twinkles — same comments as above. Contrasting dark foliage.

Minette — similar to Elfin above. Slightly more vigorous.

Crimson, red, fuchsia, pink, orange, orchid, rose, salmon, white, scarlet, and mixed.

Fuchsia, red, rose, scarlet, mixture (all bicolors).

Orange, rose-pink, salmon, bright orange with bronze foliage, scarlet, white, and mixed.

Medium 10″-12″

Fantasia — 1½″-2″ flowers in solids and bicolors. Space plants 15″-20″. Compact. Blooms early summer till frost. Use in shaded bed, tubs, and baskets.

Futura — same comments as above. Large flowers in clear colors, free-flowering.

Ripple — rich green foliage, star-patterned bicolors.

Orange, rose, orchid, pink, mauve, red and white, orange and white, mixed.

Burgundy, red, coral, orange, orchid, pink, scarlet, white, mixed.

Bicolors, star patterns, rose, scarlet, mixed.

Tall 12″-16″

Grande — 1½″-2″ solids and bicolors. Space 18″-24″ apart in shaded beds, tubs, or baskets. Blooms early summer till frost.

Imp Series — large rounded flowers, uniform and hedge-like. Withstands sun and adverse weather.

Coral, purple, white.

Carmine, orange, pink, purple, rose, scarlet, salmon, white, mixed.

Name	Life Cycle: Period of Color	Color	Form	Propagation and Culture	Use
GOMPHRENA (Globe amaranth)	Annual. July-frost.	Red-purple: 'Buddy' (1, 4, 5) Mixed purple, white, pink ,and red. (1, 2, 4, 5, 6)	9″ 18″	Seed: Soak 3-4 days before sowing indoors in March. Cover seed, keep moist, and place flat in total darkness to germinate in 2 weeks at 65°-70° soil temperatures. Drought-resistant. Set out transplants 8″-12″ apart in full sun and well-drained dryish soil.	Use as a mass planting or border. Excellent dried flowers.
GYPSOPHILA (Baby's-breath)	Annual. Perennial. June-Oct.	White: 'Covent Garden' (1, 2, 4, 5, 6) 'Double Snow Flake' (1, 4, 5) Rose: Repens 'rosea' (1, 2, 4, 5)	2′, bushy. 3′ 6″, trailing.	Seed: Annuals and perennials are sown indoors in Mar.-Apr. Cover seed lightly, keep moist, and maintain 70°-80° in soil to germinate in 10 days (perennials may take longer). Set out transplants 15″-18″ apart in full sun and well-drained humusy soil. Cut back plants before seed forms. Note: It is best to sow perennial types direct in peat pots as they resist transplanting.	Filler plant, effective with calendulas and petunias.
HELIOTROPE	Perennial grown as an annual. Summer.	Violet: 'Marine' (1, 2 ,4, 5)	1′-2′ high.	Seed: Sow indoors early spring. Cover seed lightly, keep moist, and maintain 70° in soil to germinate in 25 days. Set out transplants 12″-18″ apart in full sun, 12″-15″ apart in most well-drained soils.	Very fragrant. For rock garden or border. Does not cut well.
HEMEROCALLIS (Daylily)	Perennial. June-Aug.	Early — Rose-red: 'Magic Dawn' (2) Midseason — Red: 'Autumn Red' (2) Yellow: 'Sunshine Song' (2) Late — Purple: 'Black Magic' (2) Many more colors and bicolors.	36″ high. 39″ high. 28″-30″ high. 38″ high.	Seed: Sow indoors March. Cover lightly, keep moist, and maintain 70° soil to germinate in 2-3 weeks. From seed to flower: second year. Set out plants 24″-36″ apart in sun or partial shade in humus-enriched soil. Keep moist and divide crowded plants in early spring or late fall. To grow from divisions see page 92.	Border with iris, dusty-miller, red-hot-poker, lily-of-the-Nile. Combine with red or pink phlox, blue veronica.

Hollyhock

Iris

Lantana

Name	Life Cycle: Period of Color	Color	Form	Propagation and Culture	Use
HOLLYHOCK (Althaea)	Biennial or short-lived perennial. All summer.	Many colors. Mostly mixes of pink, red, yellow, lilac. (1, 2, 3, 4, 5, 6)	2'-5', single and double flowers on one long stalk.	Seed: Sow indoors mid-March. Cover seed ⅛", keep moist, and maintain 60° in soil to germinate in 2-3 weeks. Transplant when large enough to handle to 2¼" peat pots and shift to garden when roots emerge and weather permits. Set out 15"-20" apart in full sun and average well-drained soil. Hardy and disease-resistant. Can be sown directly outdoors as soon as soil is thoroughly warm. Often reseeds itself. Tolerates drought.	Plant as background against fence or wall. Great for hiding a metal fence. Reseeds itself readily.
HYACINTH	Perennial. Spring.	Blue, pink, white. (7)	Flowers on stalks 6"-8" high, narrow leaves.	Bulb: Plant in fall 4"-6" apart and 4"-6" deep, depending on size of bulb. Set out in full sun and a deep, rich, sandy soil.	Use in mass plantings or in pots. May be forced for indoor blooms.
HYPERICUM (St.-John's-Wort)	Perennial. Spring.	Yellow (4)	Ground cover, shrubs.	Seed: Sow indoors spring, summer. Cover lightly, keep moist, and maintain 65°-70° in soil to germinate in 3 weeks. Set out transplants in semi-shade 15"-20" apart in well-drained sandy soil. Although quite drought-resistant, plants do best with adequate water.	Cover a hillside, plant under a tree, or use in border.
IMPATIENS (Impatiens)	Annual. Summer-fall.	Various. (See chart, page 77.)	Various, (See chart, page 77.)	Seed: Sow indoors Jan.-Feb. on surface of soil mix, do not cover. Keep moist and maintain 70°-75° in soil mix during germination which takes 18-20 days. Set out transplants 15" apart in shade and a loose, fast-draining humusy soil. Keep moderately moist. To grow from cuttings see page 92. Keep an eye out for snails and sowbugs.	Very striking in hanging baskets and pots. Effective with ferns. Use under trees in filtered light.

Marigolds

Variety	Height	Flower	Type — Comments
Petite Gold	6″	Fully double 1¼″ golden flowers on compact mounds.	Petite series. French type. Series also includes 'Petite Orange,' Petite Yellow,' and 'Petite Mix.'
Petite Spry	7″	Double red with yellow crest.	
Petite Harmony	8″	Mahogany-red and orange.	
Yellow Nugget	10″-12″	Double 2¼″ flowers. Triploid.	Nugget series. Also includes: 'Orange Nugget,' 'Gold Nugget' and mixed colors.
Pumpkin Crush	10″-12″	Huge, fully double 4½″ orange blooms	Guys and Dolls series. Also offered as yellow, gold, and mixed varieties.
Gold Cupid	10″-12″	Mumlike 2½″ blooms.	Cupid series includes: orange, yellow, and mix varieties.
Spanish Brocade	10″-12″	Gold and deep red blooms.	Semidouble French bicolor. Very early.
Harvest Moon	14″	Crested 1½″ orange blooms.	Moon series also includes: 'Honey,' 'Honey Moon' (yellow). Blooms at 6″.
First Lady	18″	Double carnation type 3¼″ yellow.	Lady series. Also includes 'Gold Lady' and 'Orange Lady' and 'Primrose Lady.' Hedge type. Erect, bushy, rounded.
Naughty Marietta	18″-20″	2″ single golden yellow with red eye.	Also in this class is 'Dainty Marietta,' lower growing to 12″.
Yellow Crackerjack	30″-36″	Double carnation type 5″ blooms.	Crackerjack series. Also offered as orange, gold, and mix. Erect, bushy.
Yellow Climax	36″	Fully double carnation-type 5″ ruffled, globular blooms.	Climax series. Also includes: 'Golden,' 'Primrose' (creamy), 'Toreador' (deep orange), and mixed. Sturdy, erect, bushy.

Name	Life Cycle: Period of Color	Color	Form	Propagation and Culture	Use
IRIS	Perennial. Spring-early summer.	Many yellows, pinks, orange, purple, blue, white, and bicolors. (8)	Complex flowers classified as crested, beardless, bearded; or as German (rhizomatous) and Dutch (bulbous) iris.	Seed: Prechill seed in refrigerator 6 weeks, then remove and sow indoors, covering lightly, keeping moist and maintaining 70° in soil to germinate in 3-5 weeks. Flowers 2nd year. Set out plants 12″-18″ apart in sun in cool climates and light shade in warm climates. Rhizomes: Plant in fall or spring 2″ deep and 10″-12″ apart. Bulbs: Plant in fall 4″ deep and 4″-6″ apart. All iris take lots of water during growing season. Divide crowded clumps in late summer or fall and replant immediately.	Excellent in border or against a fence in bed. Use with red-hot-poker. Choice cut flowers.
IXIA (African corn lily)	Tender perennial. Spring.	Cream, yellow, red, orange, pink, dark centers. Flowers close at night and on cloudy days. (7)	18″-20″ Basal leaves, flowers borne on long stalks.	Corm: Plant 3″ deep and 3″-5″ apart in early fall and in a sunny well-drained sandy soil. Lift in summer, when crowded, divide, and replant in fall.	For mild-winter climates. Excellent for cutting as egg-shaped flowers are attractive even when closed.
KALANCHOE	Annual. Winter.	Red: 'Vulcan' (1, 4, 5) 'Ramona' (1, 5) 'Red Glow' (4, 5) Also rose and yellow.	Bushy. 8″ 10″-12″ 7″	Seed: Sow indoors Jan. Do not cover fine seed. Keep moist and maintain 70° to germinate in 10 days. Set out or pot up transplants in full sun and a well-drained soil. Space 10″-12″ apart. Cuttings root easily; see page 92.	Most often a pot plant for winter color in a sunny window.
LANTANA	Perennial. Year-round in frost-free areas; spring-fall elsewhere.	Orange, lavender, white. (4, 8)	Trailing or erect shrub.	Seed: Sow indoors anytime. Cover seed lightly, keep moist, and maintain 70° to germinate in 6-8 weeks. Set out transplants 12″-18″ apart in full sun in well-drained sandy soil. Heat-resistant. Allow soil to dry somewhat between thorough waterings; however, keep container plants moist. Prune hard to remove dead wood.	Use lavender variety as a ground cover, or in containers. Other varieties grow as a shrub, and can be used as a border.

Let's talk about petunias

Petunias are up on top of the list of bedding plants today. The varieties are numerous. The uses are just beginning to be explored. They will take abuse but respond beautifully to good care and pampering. First try them in a bed, then maybe a basket, then — well, then the sky's the limit. We saw them recently planted in an old wheelbarrow in a garden.

Multiflora petunias

Multifloras are more compact and uniform than grandifloras, with better weather resistance. Although the flowers are smaller, multifloras display a greater number of blooms.

Whites
Paleface — pure white with a creamy throat.
White Satin — frilled petals of pure white.
Snowberry Tart — double, pure white.

Pinks
Pink Satin — brilliant rose-pink.
Salmon Delight — light salmon-pink with double flowers.
Peppermint Tart — rose-pink veins on soft pink. Double.

Reds
Red Satin — bright red.
Red Joy — bright scarlet-red.

Purples and Blues
Plum Purple — deep purple veins on lighter purple.
Lavender Delight — Sugar Plum color, double.

Oranges and Yellow
Orange Bells — bright orange with white throat.
Summer Sun — bright yellow.

Bicolors and Mixes
Satellite — bright rose with a white star.
Starfire — scarlet and white bicolor.
Star Joy — deep rose with white star.
Plum Pudding — combination of blue-veined purple, pink, and lavender, plus yellow.
Cherry Tart — rose-pink and white. Medium-sized carnationlike double blooms.
Red and White Delight — Scarlet-red with distinct white variegation, vigorous, double.

Name	Life Cycle: Period of Color	Color	Form	Propagation and Culture	Use
LAVATERA (Annual mallow)	Annual. Aug.-frost.	Deep rose: 'Loveliness' (3, 5)	23" tall, like single holly-hocks.	Seed: Sow outdoors in May as soil warms, in full sun and well-drained soil.	Use with zinnias or sanvitalia. Tall borders.
LAVENDER (Lavandula)	Perennial. Spring-summer.	Purple: 'Vera' (2, 5, 7)	2', bushy.	Seed: Sow outdoors May (germinates slowly). Full sun and a fast-draining humusy soil. Keep moderately moist, with very little fertilizer. Prune after blooming.	Plant in or near your herb garden or with poppies and broom.
LAYIA (Tidytips)	Annual. Late spring-early summer.	Yellow with white edges. (4)	1½' bush. Daisylike flowers.	Seed: Sow indoors in early spring. Sow on surface of soil mix and do not cover seed. Keep moist and maintain 60° in the soil to germinate in 1-2 weeks. Set out transplants 9"-12" apart in full sun. Light watering.	Best in the rock garden, following California poppies. Use with ornamental grasses.
LEUCOJUM (Snowflake)	Perennial. Early spring.	White flowers with green flecks. (7)	18" long narrow leaves, 3-4 flowers per stem.	Bulb: Plant in fall 4" deep and 3"-4" apart in sun and well-drained soil. Do not disturb until crowded, then dig, divide, and replant.	Mass plantings. Use with narcissus or plant in border or by a wall. Also pot culture.
LILY (Lilium)	Perennial. Summer.	Many. (2, 4, 7)	2'-6' high stems with many slender leaves.	Bulb: Plant as soon as possible after you get them. Depth depends on variety and size of bulb. Plant in deep, well-drained humus-enriched soil 20"-30" apart in sun or filtered shade. Mulch roots and keep moist.	Mass planting along a wall, or small groups in border. Use with delphiniums, asters and marigolds. Ideal in raised beds.

Grandiflora petunias

Although tops in vigor with large ruffled flowers, grandifloras are not as prolific in flowering as multifloras. Good spreading habit lends well to planters, wall baskets, and ground cover.

Whites
White Cascade — early, large flowers. Best Cascade for planters, hanging baskets.
Old Glory White — early, large bloom, pure white.
White Magic — early, medium-large. Pure white, ruffled, compact, uniform, heavy flower production.
Snow Cloud — huge, heavy-textured, pure white blooms on dwarf compact plants.
Apollo — very early, paper white.
Bridal Bouquet — large, pure white. Fully double. Earliest and most compact habit of any white double.

Pinks
Pink Magic — bright rose-pink.
Happiness — early, large-flowered pure pink. Very uniform.

Pink Bouquet — new for 1978. Bright medium rose-pink, large double flowers. Much earlier and with a more compact habit than other pink doubles.
Blushing Maid — light double pink.

Reds
Red Cascade — brilliant deep red, extra-large flowers.
Old Glory Red — bright red, very early, medium-sized blooms, survives in hot South when other reds succumb.
Red Baron — early, vivid red.
El Toro — a bright red that's really red.
Candy Apple — early, bright scarlet.
Red Cloud — extra-large-flowered, bright red.
Red Bouquet — bright red, earlier than double reds, with same habit and performance as other Bouquets.

Purple and Blue
Sugar Daddy — large 4″ bright orchid blooms with deeper wine-red veins and shadings. Uniform. Weather-resistant.
Old Glory Blue — rich violet-blue, medium-sized bicolors, compact.
Blue Mariner — rich blue. Most dwarf of the blues. Good weather resistance.
Blue Bouquet — rich violet-blue, similar in habit and performance to Bridal Bouquet.

Other Bicolors and Mixes
Astro — red and white bicolor, large, plain-edged, slightly reflexed blooms.
Telstar — blue and white bicolor.
Fanfare — uniform blend of solid and variegated colors, with large fully double blooms, compact.

Name	Life Cycle: Period of Color	Color	Form	Propagation and Culture	Use
LILY-OF-THE-VALLEY (Convallaria)	Perennial. Spring.	White. (2, 4)	Flowers on 6″-8″ stems above 2 broad basal leaves.	Plant pips (upright, small rootstock) in Nov.-Dec. 4″-6″ apart, 1½″ deep in partial shade. Top-dress yearly with leaf mold, peat, or bark. Divide clumps every 5 years or when crowded. Need cold winter to flower again.	Use with narcissus. Mass planting best. Fine ground cover.
LINARIA (Baby snapdragon)	Annual. June-Sept.	Yellow, pink, blue, purple. 'Fairy Bouquet' (5, 6)	To 1½′	Seed: Sow outdoors in April in sunny location. Will take rather dry conditions. May tend to get a little weedy.	Best in masses. Use sweet alyssum as ground cover.
LINUM (Flax)	Perennial. Summer.	Blue: 'Perenne' (2, 3, 4, 5) Yellow: Flavum 'compactum' (4, 5)	18″ dainty plant. 6″-12″	Seed: Sow indoors in spring. Cover lightly; keep moist and maintain 60° in the soil to germinate in 2-3 weeks. Set out these drought-resistant plants 12″-15″ apart in full sun and a well-drained soil.	Use with erigeron and snow-in-summer in rock gardens.
LOBELIA	Annual. Summer.	Blue: 'Crystal Palace' (1, 2, 3, 4, 5, 6) White: 'White Lady' (1, 5) Blue: 'Blue Cascade' (1, 2, 6) 'Sapphire' with white eye (1, 2, 5, 6)	Compact, 5″. Trailing.	Seed: Sow indoors in spring. Do not cover seed, keep moist with warm water, and maintain 70°-75° in the soil to germinate in 20 days. Set out transplants 12″-15″ apart in sun or partial shade and a moist, humusy, well-drained soil. Keep moist.	Plant upright or trailing blues under trees, in rock gardens, in planter boxes with celosia or salvia. Combine trailing type with Petite marigolds in hanging basket.
LUNARIA (Money plant)	Biennial. Flowers: summer. Pods: fall.	Purple: 'Munsted Purple Giant' (2, 4) White: 'Alba' (4, 5)	2′ high. Disklike pod.	Seed: Sow indoors in early spring. Cover lightly, keep moist, and maintain 65°-75° in the soil to germinate in 10 days. Set out small plants 12″-15″ apart in an out-of-the-way spot and poor soil. Takes full sun. Tough; reseeds itself. Sow outdoors in July to germinate in 2-3 weeks.	Really just a filler. Plant in summer bed till fall comes and silver pods start dominating. Beautiful dried subject.

Marigold

Nemesia

Nicotiana

Name	Life Cycle: Period of Color	Color	Form	Propagation and Culture	Use
LUPINE (Lupinus)	Perennial. May-June.	White, yellow, pink, purple, and blue: 'Minarette' (2, 4, 5) 'Russell' (1, 2, 3, 4)	Very bushy. 2' high. 3' high.	Seed: Soak seed 24 hours, then sow indoors in spring by sowing directly in 2¼″ peat pots or pellets (difficult to transplant). Maintain constant moisture and 70°-75° in soil to germinate in 30 days. Set out small plants 12″-15″ apart in sun and a well-drained humusy soil. Thrives in cool climate. May be sown outdoors in spring when soil warms.	Fragrant flowers. For the larger garden, or in small gardens by large rocks, garden benches, and other accents. Russell Hybrids not for hot-summer areas.
MALTESE-CROSS (Lychnis)	Perennial. June only.	Red, white. (2, 4)	Bushy to 2'-2½'	Seed: Sow indoors in spring. Do not cover. Keep moist and maintain 70°-75° in the soil to germinate in 3-4 weeks. Set out transplants 15″-18″ apart in sun. Very tolerant of most soils.	Use where nothing else wants to grow. Good border plant.
MARIGOLD (Tagetes)	Annual. Summer-frost.	Yellows and oranges. (See chart, page 79.) (1, 2, 3, 4, 5, 6)	6″-36″ tall (See chart, page 79.)	Seed: May be sown indoors in spring by covering seed, keeping moist, and maintaining 75° in the soil to germinate in 7 days. May also be sown outdoors as soil warms. Sow or set out plants 12″-18″ apart in full sun and a well-drained soil.	Either in masses or one plant tucked in a corner. Great massed in large pots. Very willing to grow.
MONKEY FLOWER (Mimulus)	Annual. Summer.	Tigered and spotted flowers. (4)	12″ high. Smooth leaves.	Seed: Sow indoors in Feb. Cover lightly, keep moist, and maintain 70° in the soil. Germinates in 1-2 weeks. Set out transplants 15″-18″ apart in shade and a moist but well-drained soil.	This is a technicolor plant along edge of reflection pool or in low, wet spot with ferns. Good pot plant.
MUSCARI (Grape hyacinth)	Perennial. Spring.	Blue or white. (7)	Floppy foliage. Flowers borne on 4″-8″ stems.	Bulb: Plant 2″ deep in fall in sun or light shade, long-lived. Lift and divide when crowded.	Tuck in between or in front of daffodils.

Salvia

Salvia

| | | | | |

Dwarf 6"-10"
Red Hussar — 10". Blazing red with uniform habit for beds, foreground or edging. An early blooming variety.
Scarlet Pygmy — 6"-8". Rounded plant covered profusely with scarlet flowers.
Flarepath — 8". Plants similar to Scarlet Pygmy, but flower spikes are longer. Long lasting.

Semidwarf 12".
St. John's Fire — 12". Ideal for beds. Early and lots of scarlet red spikes.
White Fire — early 12" white. Creamy contrast with dark green foliage. Compact, bushy. Color is best in light shade. All-purpose. If grown in pots they can be brought indoors in winter and placed in a sunny window.

Medium 14"-16"
Blaze of Fire — 14"-16". Medium-early to flower, just after St. John's Fire. Uniform. Brilliant scarlet.
Red Pillar — (Hot Jazz) 14". Deep fiery red with dark bluish-green thick leaves. Bed or border.
Violet Flame — 14"-16" early, dark violet-purple. All-purpose. Mix with rudbeckia.

Semitall 18"-20"
America — 20". Bushy-green-leaved plant covered with bright red spikes. Mid-border. Background.
Firebrand — (Early Harbinger). Medium-early. 18". Long spikes of bright red. Mid-border and background.

Tall 26"-30"
Bonfire — (Clara Bedman) 26". Uniform. Medium-late. Bright scarlet-red. Good for background for foundation.
Splendens — 30". Large branching, late-flowering. Ideal for foundations and background planting. Scarlet abounds mid-summer to frost.

Name	Life Cycle: Period of Color	Color	Form	Propagation and Culture	Use
NARCISSUS (Daffodil)	Perennial. Spring.	Basically yellow with white, orange, pink, red, apricot, or cream. (7)	Flower shapes include singles, doubles, small cup, and large cup.	Bulb: Plant in early fall (solid heavy bulbs 4"-5"). Plant 5"-6" deep; smaller bulbs 4"-5" deep. Full sun best. Let foliage ripen naturally after bloom. Lift and divide clumps when blooms get small; remove only those that come away easily from mother bulb.	Solid borders are really spring eye-openers. Try in pots and containers. They stand alone beautifully but combine with other spring flowers such as candytuft and primroses.
NASTURTIUM (Tropaeolum)	Annual. Spring-summer.	Bright yellow, orange, red: 'Gleam Mixture' (1, 2, 3, 4, 5) 'Jewel Mixture'	Vigorous trailing or climbing. Extra-dwarf, hold flowers above foliage.	Seed: Soak seed overnight. Then sow outdoors after last frost. Germinates in 10 days. Best in sun in cool climates. Too rich soil causes plants to produce more leaves than flowers.	A must for cool-climate areas, but succeed even in hot Midwest. Let trail along the ground or up a wall.
NEMESIA	Annual. April-May.	Cream, orange, white, yellow, red shades. (1, 2, 4, 5, 6)	8"-10" compact dwarf.	Seed: Sow indoors Jan.-Feb., covering lightly, keeping moist, and maintaining 60°-65° in the soil to germinate in 10 days. Temperatures above 65° inhibit germination. Set out in full sun and a rich well-drained soil. Keep moist but not wet. Prefers cool climate.	Use in pots, or as an edging. Excellent bulb cover and container subject. Good with blue lobelia or violas.
NEMOPHILA (Baby-blue-eyes)	Annual. June-frost.	Blue with white center. (2, 5, 6)	3"-6" cup-shaped flowers.	Seed: Sow where it is to bloom after soil has warmed or sow indoors 8 weeks prior to last spring frost. Cover lightly, keep moist, and maintain 70° in the soil to germinate in 10-12 days. Set out transplants 12"-15" apart in sun. Quick grower. Self-sows.	Try this one in a hanging basket or use as low ground cover for tall zinnias.
NICOTIANA (Flowering tobacco)	Annual. Spring-summer.	Red: 'Idol' (4, 5, 6) White: 'Dwarf White Bedder' (4, 5, 6) Lime-green: 'Lime Sherbet' (4, 5, 6) Mixed colors: 'Sensation' Mixed (1, 3, 4, 5, 6) 'Nicki' series: pink, rose & white (1, 2, 5)	Tubular flowers. 8"-10". 12". 18". 2'-3' high. 16"-18".	Seed: Sow indoors in early March. Do not cover seed. Keep moist and maintain 70° in the soil to germinate in 15 days. Blooms 6 weeks from seed. Set out transplants 12"-18" apart in full sun or part shade and a rich, humusy, well-drained soil.	Fragrant, so plant near house — near a porch area where evening breezes catch its fragrance. Use with petunias. A real delight.

Ornithogalum

Iceland poppy

Name	Life Cycle: Period of Color	Color	Form	Propagation and Culture	Use
NIEREMBERGIA (Cupflower)	Annual. Summer.	Purple: 'Purple Robe' (1, 2, 4, 5) White (4)	6″ dwarf. 2½′ high.	Seed: Sow in early spring indoors. Cover lightly, keep moist, and maintain 70°-75° in the soil to germinate in 15 days. Blooms in 15 weeks. Set out small plants 12″-15″ apart in sun and a good soil. Retains brilliance even under strong sunlight.	Effective as edging with dusty-miller. Also for baskets or pots.
NIGELLA (Love-in-a-mist)	Annual. Late spring or early summer.	Mixtures of red, white, purple, and pink shades: 'Persian Jewels' (2, 4, 5, 6)	1′-1½′ fern-like foliage, airy looking.	While soil is cool (60°), sow seed where it is to bloom. Germinates in 2-3 weeks. Takes full sun. Doesn't need a lot of moisture.	Old-fashioned beauty in borders. Use with dwarf strawflowers.
ORNITHOGALUM (Star-of-Bethlehem)	Perennial. April-May.	White, striped green 'Nutans' 'Umbellatum' (7)	Leaves narrow to broad, tend to be floppy; flowers star-shaped in round clusters.	Plant bulbs Sept.-Oct. 2″-4″ deep depending on size; larger bulbs deeper. Sun to half shade. Good, porous soil. Lift and divide bulbs when crowded.	Fill in the daffodil bed or edge it with this one. Plant in pot by itself and enjoy its beauty.
PENSTEMON (Beard-tongue)	Perennial. Late spring-early summer.	Red, pink, purple shades. (2, 4)	1½′-2′ high, flowers on large spikes.	Seed: Sow indoors early spring or late fall. Cover seed, keep moist, and maintain 60° to germinate in 18 days. Set out transplants 12″-15″ apart in sun or partial shade. Tolerates dryish soil.	Rock garden or hillside planting.

Snapdragons

All seed catalogs carry many different snapdragon varieties. A general outline of a few common series is listed below.

Dwarf 6″-8″

Floral Carpet — 6″-8″. Compact varieties create bright spots with all colors of the rainbow. Use in border, edging, rock garden, boxes, as ground cover.

Semidwarf 12″-20″

Dwarf Butterfly types include *Little Darling* (12″), Sweetheart (12″) and *Coronette* (20″). All husky plants which require no staking. Many colors. Useful in beds, for cutting.

Intermediate 24″-30″

Butterfly Series includes *Madame Butterfly* with slightly larger florets. All are double-pleated with open-faced florets in a wide range of colors. Use in beds, border, background, for cutting.

Tall 30″-36″

Rocket — certainly the finest tall outdoor garden snapdragons. Suitable for background and cutting. Strong stems are clothed with many closely spaced florets. Available in every color. Tolerant of hot weather.

Snapdragon

Name	Life Cycle: Period of Color	Color	Form	Propagation and Culture	Use
PETUNIA	Annual. Summer-frost. (From late winter in mild climates.)	Various (See chart, pages 80-81.) (1, 2, 3, 4, 5, 6)	Various (See chart pages 80-81.)	Seed: Sow indoors in March. Do not cover seed. Keep moist and maintain 70°-80° in the soil to germinate in 10-12 days. Sow doubles in Feb. Set out transplants 12″-15″ apart in full sun and a good well-drained soil. Keep watered and fed.	One of the most popular bedding plants. Usually used alone, bordering lawn, or around tree. Grandifloras are showiest. Put them in a tub with marigolds and zinnias or in a hanging basket. Cascading varieties are very showy.
PHLOX	Annual. Early summer till frost. Perennial. Summer.	Pink, red, blue, salmon, white: 'Globe' (1, 2, 3, 5) 'Beauty' (1, 2, 3, 4, 6) 'Twinkle' (1, 2, 4, 5) Mix: 'Beltsville Beauty' (1, 4, 6, 8) *'Paniculata'*	8″ rounded plant habit. 7″ 7″ dwarf, compact. 3′ high.	Seed: Sow annual types indoors in March. Cover seed, place flat in total darkness to germinate in 10 days at 65° soil temperature. Set out in full sun 12″-18″ apart in a light, rich loam. Remove old blooms. Keep moist and cultivated. Sow perennial types indoors in spring after refrigerating seed 6 weeks. Remove and sow, covering lightly, keeping moist, and maintaining 65°-75° in the soil to germinate in 3-4 weeks. Culture as annual above. Divide every 2-3 years, replanting the young shoots from sides of clumps.	Attractive in baskets combined with browallia or lobelia. Ground cover with nicotiana or zinnias. 'Twinkle' is interesting bordering a lawn or walk. For borders, beds, edgings, to go with perennial.
PLATYCODON (Balloon flower)	Perennial. June-Aug.	Blue, white, mixed. (4, 6, 8)	24″ upright, branching stem. Star-shaped flowers.	Seed: Sow indoors in spring. Do not cover. Keep moist, maintaining 70° in the soil to germinate in 21 days. Set out 10″-12″ apart in sun or light shade (warmer areas) and good soil. Moderate water. Remove faded blooms. Protect roots from gophers. Takes 2-3 years to become established.	Border with low-growing campanulas. Looks nice with butterfly flower, dianthus, gloriosa daisy, and ajuga.
POPPY (Papaver)	Perennial. Sometimes grown as annuals.	Iceland Mix: 'Champagne Bubbles' (1, 2, 3, 4) Oriental Mix: colors include red, orange, salmon, pink. (1, 2, 3, 4, 5, 6)	1′ rosette with flowers on stalks 2½′-3′ high.	Seed: Sow outdoors in May after soil has warmed or sow indoors Apr.-May. Do not cover seed. Place flat in total darkness to germinate in 10 days at 70° soil temperatures. Keep soil mix moist but not wet. Set out small plants in sun and ordinary soil. Keep watered but do not fertilize. Remove faded blooms to prolong flowering. Protect young plants from birds. Plant divisions of Oriental poppies.	Excellent bedding. Spring-flowering plant. Use with pansies or calendulas; Oriental poppies are striking planted by themselves.

Portulaca

Rudbeckia

Ranunculus

Name	Life Cycle: Period of Color	Color	Form	Propagation and Culture	Use
PORTULACA (Moss rose)	Annual. Early summer till frost.	'Sunglo' series: white, cream, gold, yellow, pink, rose, red, orange, orchid. (1, 2, 4, 5, 6)	Low-growing, spreading to 18". Double flowers resemble small rose.	Seed: Sow in 2¼" peat pots or pellets indoors in early spring. Do not cover seed. Keep moist and maintain 70° in soil to germinate in 10 days. Set out transplants 9"-15" apart in full sun and a well-drained sandy loam. Thrives in hot, dry conditions. May also be sown outdoors after soil has warmed. Blooms in 8 weeks.	Ground cover in rock garden or sloping hillside. Try some in a hanging basket. Ideal drought-resistant plant.
PRIMULA (Primrose)	Annual. Jan.-April. Perennial. Spring-June.	'Rhinepearl' series: carmine, white, rose, mixed. (1, 4) 'Laser' series: scarlet, yellow, myosotis blue, white, pink, all white with yellow eye. 'Pacific Giants' (3, 7)	Base-branching, flowers borne close to foliage. Rosette with short, strong flower stems. 10".	Seed: Sow annual types indoors June-Sept. Do not cover seed. Keep moist and maintain 70° to germinate in 3-4 weeks. Set out small plants 12" apart in humusy, moist but well-drained soil. Sun to partial shade. Thrives in cool, moist climates. Does not tolerate poor drainage. Sow perennial types indoors in Aug. same as above.	Edging plant for lawn area. Definitely a plant to be used with others, such as candytuft, pansies, calendulas, lettuce, and violas. May be massed in large bed, looks nice edging a wooded path.
RANUNCULUS	Perennial. Spring.	Yellow, orange, red, white, pink (Tecolote strain). (7)	Up to 18" Semidouble to fully double.	Tubers: Plant Nov. or mid-Feb. Set tubers (prongs down) 2" deep, 6"-8" apart. Takes full sun and moderate water. Tubers rot if overwatered.	In masses a sensational show of color. Use with snapdragons, pansies, and daffodils. For mild-winter zones. In pots anywhere.
RUDBECKIA (Gloriosa daisy)	Perennial. Summer-frost.	Orange, dark eye: 'Marmalade' (1, 3, 5, 6) Yellow, brown eye: 'Double Gloriosa Daisies' (1, 2, 3, 4, 5, 6) Mixtures-yellow, mahogany-red: 'Rustic' (1, 4, 6) 'Single Gloriosa Daisy' (1, 2, 3, 4 ,5) 'Pinwheel' (2, 4, 5)	Daisylike flowers. 18"-22" tall. 3' high. 18"-22" high. 3' high. 2½' high.	Seed: Sow indoors Feb.-Mar. Cover lightly, keeping moist, and maintaining 70° in the soil to germinate in 3 weeks. Set out 15"-18" apart in full sun and good well-drained soil. Does not tolerate soggy soil. Hardy. May be sown outdoors in spring when soil warms.	Showy in bed among other green plants. Fine, long-lasting cut flower. Use with maltese-cross, butterfly flower, bellflower.

Let's talk about sweet alyssum

Alyssum is probably one of the most used and most versatile accent plants today. You can plant it just about anywhere. If you've got a vacant spot, fill it with alyssum. The color appears quickly and lasts all season. Use it with vegetables to liven them up. Hang it, box it, carpet a walk, cover a bed. The uses are endless. One might say it's the best friend all the other flowers have.

Sweet alyssum

Extra-Dwarf 3″

New Carpet of Snow — uniform spreading habit. 15″ across and 3″-4″ tall. The dainty white stays clear all season.

Pastel Carpet — a low-growing, uniform, 3″ plant which spreads 12″-15″ and is covered early with a profusion of white, cream-yellow, rose, dark purple, and pink in mixture.

Snow Cloth — a 3″ refined strain of Carpet of Snow and 10 days earlier. The 12″ spread is covered with masses of the purest white.

Tiny Tim — an extremely early 3″ snow-white-flowered plant.

Dwarf 4″

Oriental Night — compact 4″ plant of the deepest color to date. A rich dark violet-purple. Plant habit similar to that of Tiny Tim. The flowers have a small white center. Striking!

Rosie O'Day — spreading 10″-12″, this low, 4″, heat-resistant plant is ideal as ground cover or for edging. Pleasantly fragrant with a habit similar to that of Tiny Tim. The lavendar-rose blends beautifully with white.

Royal Carpet — a 4″ violet-purple which spreads 10″-12″ and flowers freely.

Snowdrift — outstanding, 4″, uniform. Compact, yet spreading habit, not quite as vigorous as Carpet of Snow but with slightly larger pure white flowers.

Name	Life Cycle: Period of Color	Color	Form	Propagation and Culture	Use
SALPIGLOSSIS (Painted-tongue) (Velvet flower)	Annual. July-Sept.	Scarlet, yellow, purple, orange, blue, marbled and penciled contrasting color. (1, 3, 4, 6)	2½′ bushy, compact.	Seed: Sow indoors in Feb.-Mar. Cover seed, place flat in total darkness to germinate in 14 days. Keep soil moist and a constant 70°-75°. Set out transplants in sun and space 12″-15″ apart in a rich, well-drained soil.	Showy backdrop for sanvitalia or low-growing zinnias. One of finest cut flowers.
SALVIA (Scarlet sage)	Annual. June-frost.	Red shades and others. (See chart, page 83.) (1, 2, 4, 5, 6)	8″-30″ high. (See chart, page 83.)	Seed: Sow indoors Feb.-Apr. Do not cover seed. Keep moist and maintain 70° in the soil to germinate in 12-15 days. Set out 12″-15″ apart in sun or light shade and good humusy soil. Does not tolerate cold temperature. May be sown outdoors after soil has warmed.	Plant a whole section of bed for spectacular show. For edging or background, depending on variety. Great with other annuals.
SANVITALIA (Creeping zinnia)	Annual. Summer.	Yellow, dark centers. (1, 4, 5)	6″ trailing habit, daisy-like flowers.	Seed: Sow indoors in spring. Do not cover seed. Keep moist and maintain 70° in the soil to germinate in 7 days. Set out plants in sun and well-drained soil. Space 8″-10″.	Pretty little ground cover, creeping in and out of vegetable garden or flower bed. Ideal in window box.
SAPONARIA (Soapwort)	Perennial. Late spring-early summer.	Pink. (4, 6)	12″ trailing habit, spreading 3′.	Seed: Sow indoors in spring. Cover lightly, keep moist and maintain 60° in the soil to germinate in 2-3 weeks. Set out in sun, any soil, and keep moist in dry weather. Easy to grow. Space 12″.	Nice ground cover in a hard-to-handle area.

Schizanthus

Verbena

Sweet alyssum

Zinnia

Name	Life Cycle: Period of Color	Color	Form	Propagation and Culture	Use
SCABIOSA (Pincushion flower)	Annual. July-frost. Perennial. Mid-summer to frost.	Rose, purple, blue, white. (1, 2, 4, 5) Mixture, white to deep blue: 'Caucasica' (1, 4, 5)	3' high. Flowers cushionlike. 2½' high.	Seed: Sow annual types indoors in Mar.-Apr. Cover lightly, keep moist, and maintain 70° in the soil to germinate in 12 days. Sow perennials in spring as above at 60° to germinate in 18 days. Set young plants out in sun. Easy to grow. Space 12" apart.	Great cut flowers. Pastel shades good foil for brighter colors.
SCHIZANTHUS (Butterfly flower) (Poor-man's orchid)	Annual. Jan.-Apr. in mild-winter areas. Summer, elsewhere.	White, purple, pink, red, bicolors with contrasting markings. 'Giant Hybrids Mixed' (2) 'Hit parade' (4)	18" tall. 12" compact.	Seed: Sow indoors in Aug.-Jan. Do not cover seed and place flat in total darkness to germinate in 15 days at 60° soil temperature. Keep moist. Set out young plants 12" apart in partial shade. Sensitive to frost or heat.	Combine with primula and cineraria. Use in pot in patio area in California or cool greenhouse. Not for zones with very hot summers.
SCILLA (Bluebells)	Perennial. Spring.	Blue, purple, white. (7)	Basal leaves, bell-shaped flowers.	Bulb: Plant 4" to 6" deep in sun or light shade.	Plant around deciduous trees, or as a border.
SNAPDRAGON (Antirrhinum)	Perennial usually treated as annual. Spring-early summer.	Many and multiple. (See chart, page 85.) (1, 2, 3, 4, 5, 6)	Many and various. (See chart, page 85.)	Seed: Sow indoors in early spring to late summer after prechilling 5 days in refrigerator. Remove, do not cover seed, keep moist, and maintain 70° in the soil to germinate in 1-2 weeks. Transplant when large enough to handle to 2¼" peat pots. Pinch lightly after plants have 3-4 sets of leaves to induce branching. Set out 8"-12" apart (spring in cold regions and fall in warm regions) in full sun and well-drained, humusy soil. Keep moist but avoid overhead watering to deter rust.	Informal mass plantings best. Wide range of colors makes any dull area a real eye-opener. Gives vertical accent. Use with nicotiana, baby-blue-eyes or sweet alyssum as ground cover.

Verbena

Spreading types 8"-12"
Ruffled White — 10", pleasantly scented. Pure white. Semidouble flowers.
Ruffled pink — 10" soft salmon-pink. Semidouble flowers.

Sparkle types 8"-12"
Amethyst — 8" mid-blue, compact, free-flowering.
Blaze — 6"-8". Bright scarlet without an eye. Compact, free-flowering.
Crystal — 8" large-flowered snow-white.
Dazzle — 6"-8". Compact, solid scarlet-red.
Delight — 8". Coral-pink suffused salmon.
Sparkle — 8". Deep reddish-purple with a white eye.

Florist's plants
Ideal florist Mixture — 8" tall, spreading to 18". Wide range of colors from white to scarlet, and pink to purple, each with a bit of white in the center. Low-growing, early, free-flowering plant with a spreading habit.

Upright types 8"-10"
Rainbow Mixture — 8"-10". Early plant in a wide range of colors. Erect semidwarf plants lend themselves nicely to pots, planters and borders.
Regalia Mixture — 10". Includes many bright pastels. Dwarf, compact, and very uniform. All season.

Name	Life Cycle: Period of Color	Color	Form	Propagation and Culture	Use
STATICE (Limonium)	Perennial. Spring-summer.	Purple: 'Latifolia' (2, 4) White: 'Iceberg' (1, 5) Yellow: 'Gold Coast' (1, 5) Rose: 'American Beauty' (1, 5)	Bushy. 2' high. 2½' high. 2½' high. 2½' high.	Seed: Sow indoors in early spring. Cover lightly, keep moist, and maintain 70° in the soil to germinate in 15-20 days. Seed may also be sown outdoors after soil has warmed. Set out small plants 12"-15" apart in sun and a well-drained soil. Tolerates heat.	Good in old-fashioned gardens, or rock gardens. Plant violet ones among yellow marigolds. Flowers excellent for cut use and drying.
STOCK (Matthiola)	Annual. Spring-summer.	Mixed white, pink, yellow, red, blue: 'Trysomic 7 Weeks' (1, 2, 4, 5, 6) 'Dwarf 10 Weeks' (1, 2, 4, 5, 6) 'Giant Imperial' (2, 4, 5, 6)	15" double. 12". 26".	Seed: Sow indoors in mid-Feb. Cover lightly, keep moist, and maintain 65°-75° in the soil to germinate in 2 weeks. Transplant when large enough to handle to 2¼" peat pots and grow on at cool 45°-50° temperatures, if possible. Set out transplants 12" apart in light, fertile soil. Some varieties are weather-resistant; however, all thrive in cool weather.	Scent is heavenly. A must for color in garden. Mass plantings most effective. Good as cut flowers.
STRAWFLOWER (Helichrysum)	Annual. Summer.	Wide range. Dwarf mix (2, 3, 4, 5, 6) 'Monstrosum' mix (1, 2, 3, 4, 5, 6)	Bushy. 12" high. 3' high.	Seed: Sow indoors in Mar. Do not cover seed. Keep moist and maintain 70° in the soil to germinate in 7 days. Set out transplants in full sun. Space 15"-18" apart. Good for hillsides or dry level places. Harvest in September for drying.	Beautiful cut flower and lasting dry flower. Use with lunaria in mass planting.
SUNFLOWER (Helianthus)	Annual. Late summer-fall.	Yellow: 'Sungold' (2, 4, 6) 'Teddy Bear' (2, 4, 5, 6) White: 'Italian White' (4, 5)	6' high. 3' bushy. 4' high.	Seed: Sow outdoors after soil has warmed in spring. Germinates in 2-3 weeks. Set in full sun and any garden soil. Not for the tidy garden. May also be sown indoors 4 weeks prior to setting out by sowing in 2¼" peat pots or pellets. Keep moist and maintain 70° in the soil to germinate in 5-7 days.	Plant along fence or make your own annual screen by planting close together to enclose yard. Use tall zinnias or marigolds to conceal base.
SWEET ALYSSUM (Lobularia)	Annual. June-frost.	Whites, violets and pinks. (See chart, page 87.) (1, 2, 3, 4, 5)	Low branching, trailing plant to 1'. (See chart, page 87.)	Seed: Sow indoors in Mar.-Apr. Do not cover seed. Keep moist and maintain 70° to germinate in 8 days. Set out small plants in sun or light shade. Tolerates moist well-drained soils. Space 6"-10" apart.	Many uses; try as ground cover or mat for upright lobelia. Plant in clumps between rocks in rock garden. Throw seed in bed for surprising natural effect.

Viola and pansy

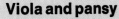

Violas

Arkwright Ruby — bright maroon with dark center.
Blue Perfection — large medium blue.
Chantreyland — extra large apricot color.
Lutea Splendens — golden yellow.
White Perfection — pure white.
Jersey Gem — large violet blue.
Johnny-Jump-Ups — smaller.
　Blue Elf — deep violet and light blue with gold eye.
　Helen Mount — combination of violet, lavender, canary-yellow, narrow, bushy foliage.

Pansy

Golden Champion — largest-flowered clear golden yellow.
Imperial Giants Blue — light lavender-blue to violet with small bright yellow eye. 2½", very uniform and compact.
Sunny Boy — bright yellow with blotch.
Majestic Giants — flowers to 4" with conspicuous blotch. Blue, purple, red, rose, bronze, scarlet, white with blotch, yellow with blotch.
Color Carnival — American-produced strain of Swiss Giants. Large flowers, many colors, typical pansy face.
Masquerade — California strain of Steele Jumbo with better color range.
Roggli Swiss Giants — huge flowers on long stems. All have dark blotch except Jungfrau and Monch.
　Alpengluhn — mahogany-red.
　Blumlisalp — raspberry-rose.
　Eiger — yellow.

Grimsel — mid-blue, lighter and earlier than Thunersee.
Hohenfeur — orange.
Jungfrau — ivory.
Monch — golden yellow.
Thunersee — blue.
Steele Jumbo — mixture.

Clear Colors:
Berna — dark, velvety-blue.
Coronation Gold — golden yellow.
Delft Blue — porcelain-blue.
Paper White — Pure white with a yellow eye.
True Blue — light mid-blue shades.

Dark centers:
Raspberry Rose — shades of pink.
Rhinegold — yellow.
Lake of Thun — mid-blue.

Name	Life Cycle: Period of Color	Color	Form	Propagation and Culture	Use
SWEET PEA (Lathyrus)	Annual. Spring-Summer.	Blue, pink, yellow, purple, white. 'Royal Mix' 'Multiflora Mix' 'Jet Set' (1, 2, 3, 4, 5, 6)	Vinelike, trailing.	Seed: Soak 24-48 hours, then sow indoors, covering seed, placing flat in total darkness and germinating in 15 days at 55° soil temperature. Sow outside as early as soil can be worked in colder regions or in fall in warmer areas. Set out in sun and give adequate water. Not particular about soil. Needs support.	For covering a wall or fence. Grown on a barrier or screen, adds color to vegetable garden.
THUNBERGIA (Black-eyed Susan)	Perennial grown as annual. Summer.	Yellow and orange, black eyes: 'Alata' (1, 2, 3, 4, 5, 6)	Trailing vine.	Seed: Sow indoors in March. Cover seed. Keep moist and maintain 70° soil to germinate in 12 days (may be erratic in germinating). Pot up or set out small plants 12"-15" apart in sun and humusy soil with adequate moisture. May also be sown outdoors when soil warms.	For hanging basket, or let it climb a fence or post.
TORENIA (Wishbone flower)	Annual. Late spring-early summer.	Deep blue with violet, yellow blotch on lip: 'Fournieri' (2)	8" compact, bushy. Flowers like miniature gloxinia.	Seed: Sow indoors in Feb. Cover lightly, keep moist and maintain 70° in the soil to germinate in 15 days. Set out small transplants in shade or semishade and a well-drained humusy soil. Space 10"-12".	Nice in borders, pots, or window boxes. Plant in mass in filtered sun.
TULIPS (Tulipa)	Perennial. March-May.	Whites, pinks, yellows, reds, oranges, some bicolors. (7)	Single and double flowers in many forms.	Bulb: Plant in Oct. Nov. 2½ times as deep as they are wide. Store at 40°-50° for 6-8 weeks before planting in mild-winter areas. Takes full sun and sandy soil.	Plant in masses for outstanding color show or combine with candytuft or pansies.
VERBENA	Perennial grown as annual. Spring-summer.	Various (See chart, page 89.) (1, 2, 4, 5)	Spreading and upright. (See chart, page 89.)	Seed: Sow indoors in Feb. Cover seed lightly, keep barely moist, place flat in total darkness to germinate in 20 days at 65°-70° soil temperatures. Set out small plants in sun and a well-drained sandy soil. Drought-resistant and thrives in warm areas.	Nice edging for bed. Good in pots or hanging baskets. Use around yarrow or with dusty-miller.

Zinnias

Height 6"-8"

Thumbelina — yellow, pink, lavender, orange, scarlet, white. 1½" flowers in mounds, June to frost. Space 6" apart in borders.

Height 10"-14"

Peter Pan Series — pink, scarlet, plum, orange. 3" double, flattened, informal flowers on mound-shaped plant. Space 12" apart for beds or borders. Good for cutting.

Cupid Mixture — 12". Small 1" double flower in mixed colors. Space and use as above.

Button Series — Pink, red, yellow, white. 12" tall plants with 1½" double flowers on long stems for cutting, borders, beds. Space 12" apart.

Height 18"-24"

Liliput — (Pompon) 2" crimson, rose, pink, yellow, white, and lavender rounded flowers on bushy plants. Use for cutting, beds, foreground. Flowers early summer to frost. Space 12".

Height 24"-30"

Ruffles — scarlet and pink to 2¼". Round flowers. Upright. Space 12". Good for cutting and background. Early summer to frost.

Whirligig — 3½"-4½" bicolored patterns adorn 24"-30" upright plants. Ideal for background or cutting. Early summer to frost.

Pumila — (Cut and Come Again) 2"-2½" flowers of canary-yellow, fireball-red, pink, salmon-rose, and white (Snowball) on 24"-30" mounded plants.

Height 30"-36"

Giant Cactus Flower 5" flowers on 30" stems. Space 24" apart. Ivory, rose-pink, tangerine, two-toned bright red and deep scarlet-red. Early summer to frost. For background cutting, and mass plantings.

State Fair — 30"-36". Range of scarlet, yellow, purple, orange, and pink. Early summer to frost, with lots of 5" dahlia-type flowers. Use for cutting and in background, beds. Space 26".

Dahlia-Flowered — 4"-5". (Giant Mammoth) Dahlia type in red, chartreuse, purple, and yellow. Space 24".

Zenith — 5"-6" red, rose, orange, yellow cactus type. Space 24".

Name	Life Cycle: Period of Color	Color	Form	Propagation and Culture	Use
VERONICA (Speedwell)	Perennial. Spring.	Blue, pink: 'Spicata' mixed (4, 5) Blues: 'Repens' (4) 'Incana' (4)	2', bushy. 2" 9", trailing.	Seed: Sow outdoors where it is to bloom. Germinates in 2-3 weeks. Plant in a sunny location. Not really particular about soil. Should have good drainage.	Plant tall types among nicotiana. Trailing types can be used in front of geraniums.
VINCA (Periwinkle)	Annual. Summer-frost.	White: Little Blanche' (1, 2, 4) 'Little Bright Eye' (red eye) (1, 2, 4) Pink: 'Little Delicata' (red eye) (1, 2, 4) 'Little Pinkie' (1, 2, 4, 5) Mixes	Dwarf, compact. Bush type to 1½'.	Seed: Sow indoors in Feb. Cover seed lightly, keep moist, and place flat in total darkness to germinate in 15 days at 70°-75° soil temperatures. Set out transplants in full sun. Thrives under hot, dry conditions and sensitive to overwatering and cold temperatures. Slow grower. Quite free from insects and diseases. Space 10"-12" apart.	Use as a ground cover or plant in a hanging basket. It can stand on its own or combine with other plants, such as edging a salvia bed. Often reseeds.
VIOLA (Violet, pansy)	Perennials. Annuals. Winter-summer, depending on climate.	Many (See chart, page 90.) (1, 2, 3, 4, 5, 6; perennial violets, 8)	Many (See chart, page 90.)	Seed: Sow perennial violets indoors in Jan.-Feb. Cover lightly, place seed flat in total darkness, keep moist and germinate in 2-3 weeks at 65° soil temperatures. Set out 8"-12" apart in full sun or shade and a rich, moist, humus-enriched soil. Tough plants. Sow annual types (violas and pansies) indoors in Dec.-Jan. or in Aug. to germinate as above in 10 days at 65°-75° Culture same as above.	One of the most popular bedding, border, and pot plants. Use just about anywhere with just about anything.
ZINNIAS	Annual. Summer-early fall.	Various (See chart, page 91.) (1, 2, 3, 4, 5, 6)	Various 10"-3' (See chart, page 91.)	Seed: Sow indoors in Mar.-Apr. Cover lightly, keep moist, and maintain 70° in soil to germinate in 7 days. Transplant as soon as large enough to handle to 2¼" peat pots and set out when roots emerge from pot walls and when weather permits. Grow on after transplanting at cooler (60°-65°) temperatures to avoid yellow leaves. Set out in moist, well-drained, humusy soil 12"-18" apart in full sun.	Popular and very versatile. Lots of different colors and forms. Use in beds with marigolds, edge with dusty-miller, or tuck in among your vegetables.

How to grow plants from cuttings or divisions

Cuttings. To propagate a plant by cuttings simply snip off a piece of plant material 3" to 5" long, cutting just below where a leaf joins the stem. Remove all but two sets of leaves. (For best rooting, dip cutting into a rooting hormone first.) Place into a growing medium such as vermiculite, packaged mix, or sphagnum moss, and keep moist. Cover with plastic for a few days to maintain humidity. Repot into larger pots after roots fill original container. Many plants are easily started from cuttings and won't present any problem if these rules are followed: Reduce leaf area by snipping some large leaves off and reduce size of remaining large ones; young growth usually will root easier than old growth; remove flowers or flower buds on cuttings.

Divisions. Divide clumps of perennials when they get crowded. Some grow so fast they might need dividing every two years (such as yarrow). Others will need attention only every three years or more (tritoma). Be guided by flower production. When it decreases dividing the plants is in order.

Dig up a whole clump and do it gently, usually by prying it up with a spade from just one side. Separate plants by pulling apart (daylilies), or by cutting (iris). Remove dead foliage from plants and discard old woody centers (chrysanthemums).

Early spring is the time to divide the plants that bloom in the summer and fall; those that bloom in the spring and early summer should be divided in the fall.

By any other name —

You may know it as . . .	How it's listed in the chart
A	
Achimenes	Achimenes
African corn lily	Ixia
African daisy	Dimorphotheca
African lily	Agapanthus, or Dimorphotheca
Alkanet	Anchusa
Alpine violet	Cyclamen
Althaea	Hollyhock
Alumroot	Coralbells
Amethyst flower	Browallia
Angel-wings	Caladium
Annual aster	Aster
Antirrhinum	Snapdragon
Aquilegia	Columbine
Aurinia	Alyssum
Avens	Geum
B	
Baby-blue-eyes	Nemophila
Baby's-breath	Gypsophilia
Baby snapdragon	Linaria
Bachelor's-button	Cornflower
Balloon flower	Platycodon
Balsam	Impatiens
Barbados lily	Amaryllis
Basket-of-gold	Alyssum
Beard-tongue	Penstemon
Bellflower	Campanula
Bellis	English daisy
Bitter Indian	Nasturtium
Black-eyed Susan	Rudbeckia
Black-eyed Susan vine	Thunbergia
Blanket flower	Gaillardia
Bluebell	Scilla
Bluebottle	Cornflower
Blue-buttons	Vinca
Blue-devil	Echium
Blue marguerite	Felicia
Brookline	Veronica
Bugloss	Anchusa
Bush violet	Browallia
Busy Lizzy	Impatiens
Buttercup	Ranunculus
Butterfly flower	Schizanthus
C	
California poppy	Eschscholzia
Calla lily	Calla lily
Calliopsis	Coreopsis
Callistephus	Aster

You may know it as . . .	How it's listed in the chart
Canterbury-bells	Campanula
Cape daisy	Dimorphotheca
Cape marigold	Dimorphotheca
Carnation	Dianthus
China aster	Aster
China bellflower	Platycodon
Chinese woolflower	Celosia
Cigar plant	Cuphea
Clock vine	Thunbergia
Cockscomb	Celosia
Coneflower	Rudbeckia
Convallaria	Lily-of-the-valley
Coralbells	Coralbells
Corn flag	Gladiolus
Corn poppy	Poppy
Creeping zinnia	Sanvitalia
Crowfoot	Ranunculus
Cupflower	Nierembergia
Cupid's-bower	Achimenes
D	
Daffodil	Narcissus
Daylily	Hemerocallis
Dove's dung	Ornithogalum
Dusty-miller	Dusty-miller
E	
Elephant's-ear	Caladium
Eleven-o'clock	Portulaca
Everlasting	Strawflower
F	
Farewell-to-spring	Clarkia
Feverfew	Chrysanthemum
Firecracker plant	Cuphea
Flag	Iris
Flax	Linum
Fleabane	Erigeron
Fleur-de-lis	Iris
Flossflower	Ageratum
Flowering tobacco	Nicotiana
Forget-me-not	Forget-me-not
Foxglove	Digitalis
G	
Gillyflower	Stock
Globe amaranth	Gomphrena
Gloriosa daisy	Rudbeckia
Gloxinia	Gloxinia
Godetia	Clarkia
Goldentuft	Alyssum
Grape hyacinth	Muscari

You may know it as . . .	How it's listed in the chart
H	
Heart-of-Jesus	Caladium
Helianthus	Sunflower
Helichrysum	Strawflower
Heuchera	Coralbells
Honesty	Lunaria
I	
Iberis	Candytuft
Iceland poppy	Poppy
Immortelle	Strawflower
Indian cress	Nasturtium
J	
Japanese pansy	Achimenes
Jasmine tobacco	Nicotiana
Jerusalem-cross	Maltese-cross
Jewelweed	Impatiens
Joseph's coat	Amaranthus
Johnny-jump-up	Viola
Jonquil	Narcissus
L	
Lady's-eardrops	Fuchsia
Larkspur	Delphinium
Lathyrus	Sweet pea
Lavendula	Lavender
Leather flower	Clematis
Lillium	Lily
Limonium	Statice
Lily-of-the-field	Anemone
Lily-of-the-Nile	Agapanthus
Lily-of-the-valley	Lily-of-the-valley
Lobularia	Sweet alyssum
London-pride	Maltese-cross
Love-in-a-mist	Nigella
Love-lies-bleeding	Amaranthus
Lupinus	Lupine
Lychnis	Maltese-cross
M	
Madwort	Alyssum
Magic flower	Achimenes
Mallow (annual)	Lavatera
Maltese-cross	Maltese-cross
Marigold	Marigold
Marsh mallow	Hollyhock
Marsh rosemary	Statice
Matricaria	Chrysanthemum
Matthiola	Stock

You may know it as . . .	How it's listed in the chart
Mimulus	Monkey flower
Money plant	Lunaria
Monkey-faced pansy	Achimenes
Monkey flower	Monkey flower
Moonwort	Lunaria
Moss rose	Portulaca
Mother-in-law-plant	Caladium
Mother's-tears	Achimenes
Mountain-garland	Clarkia
Mountain-pride	Penstemon
Mum	Chrysanthemum
Myosotis	Forget-me-not
Myrtle	Vinca

N

Nap-at-noon	Ornithogalum
Nasturtium	Nasturtium
Nut orchid	Achimenes

O

Orchid pansy	Achimenes
Oriental poppy	Poppy
Ornamental onion	Allium

P

Painted daisy	Chrysanthemum
Painted-tongue	Salpiglossis
Palm-Beach-bells	Kalanchoe
Pansy	Viola
Papaver	Poppy
Pelargonium	Geranium
Periwinkle	Vinca
Persian Violet	Cyclamen
Pincushion flower	Scabiosa
Pink	Dianthus
Plum flower	Celosia
Pocketbook flower	Calceolaria
Poor-man's orchid	Schizanthus
Pot-of-gold	Coreopsis
Pot marigold	Calendula
Pouch flower	Calceolaria
Primrose	Primula

You may know it as . . .	How it's listed in the chart
Prince's-feather	Amaranthus
Pussy-foot	Ageratum
Pyrethrum	Chrysanthemum

R

Ramona	Salvia
Red-white-and-blue flower	Cuphea
Rock-cress	Arabis
Rose-of-the-rockery	Geum

S

Sage	Salvia
St.-John-wort	Hypericum
Sapphire flower	Browallia
Satin flower	Lunaria, Clarkia
Scabiosa	Scabiosa
Scarlet-lightning	Maltese-cross
Scorpion grass	Forget-me-not
Sea lavender	Statice
Sea pink	Armeria
Senecio	Cineraria
Shasta daisy	Chrysanthemum
Shirley poppy	Poppy
Shrub verbena	Lantana
Silver-dollar plant	Lunaria
Sinningia	Gloxinia
Slipper flower	Calceolaria
Slipperwort	Calceolaria
Snapweed	Impatiens
Snowflake	Leucojum
Snow-in-summer	Cerastium
Soapwort	Saponaria
Sowbread	Cyclamen
Speedwell	Veronica
Spider flower	Cleome
Spurred snapdragon	Linaria
Squill	Scilla
Star-of-Bethlehem	Ornithogalum
Statice	Statice
Stock	Stock
Storksbill	Geranium
Strawflower	Strawflower
Summer forget-me-not	Anchusa

You may know it as . . .	How it's listed in the chart
Summer snowflake	Ornithogalum
Sunflower	Sunflower
Sun plant	Portulaca
Swan river daisy	Brachycome
Sweet alyssum	Sweet alyssum
Sweet pea	Sweet pea
Sweet William	Dianthus
Sword lily	Gladiolus

T

Tagetes	Marigold
Tassel flower	Amaranthus
Thrift	Armeria
Tickseed	Coreopsis
Tidy-tips	Layia
Toadflax	Linaria
Touch-me-not	Impatiens
Tower-of jewels	Echium
Transvaal daisy	Gerbera
Tropaeolum	Nasturtium
Turnsole	Heliotrope

V

Vase vine	Clematis
Velvet flower	Salpiglossis
Vervain	Verbena
Violet	Viola
Violet slipper	Gloxinia
Viper's bugloss	Echium
Virgin's-bower	Clematis

W Y Z

Wallflower	Cheiranthus
Widow's-tears	Achimenes
Wild fennel	Nigella
Windflower	Anemone
Wishbone flower	Torenia
Yarrow	Achillea
Zantedeschia	Calla lily

Plants by color and height

Orange	Extra-dwarf up to 8"	Dwarf 8"-14"			Rudbeckia	Poppy
	Crocus	Calceolaria	Narcissus	Coreopsis	Zinnia	Salpiglossis
	Gazania	California	Nasturtium	Cosmos		Sunflower
	Marigold	poppy	Zinnia	Freesia		Thunbergia
	Nemesia	Dimorphotheca		Gaillardia	Tall	(vine)
	Portulaca	Gaillardia	Medium 16"-24"	Impatiens	30" or more	Tithonia
	Sanvitalia	Gerbera	Calendula	Ixia	Canna	
		Marigold	Cheiranthus	Lantana	Gloriosa daisy	
			Chrysanthemum	Marigold	Lily	
				Poppy	Marigold	

Blue	Extra-dwarf up to 8"				Stock	Iris
	Ageratum	Torenia	Cornflower	Aster	Veronica	Lupine
	Campanula	Verbena	Gloxinia	Cornflower		Salpiglossis
	Crocus	Veronica	Iris	Delphinium		Scabiosa
	Forget-me-not		Lychnis	Felicia	Tall	Sweet pea (vine)
	Hyacinth	Dwarf 8"-14"	Petunia	Forget-me-not	30" or more	
	Iris	Achimenes	Primrose	Freesia	Anchusa	
	Lobelia	Ageratum	Viola	Iris	Aster	
	Muscari	Anchusa		Linaria	Campanula	
	Nemophila	Anemone	Medium 16"-24"	Linum	Clematis (vine)	
	Phlox	Aster	Agapanthus	Lupine	Cornflower	
	Scilla	Brachycome	Anchusa	Nigella	Delphinium	
		Browallia	Anemone	Platycodon	Echium	
				Salvia		

White

Extra-dwarf up to 8"
Ageratum, Arabis, Begonia, Campanula, Candytuft, Cerastium, Convallaria, Crocus, Dianthus, Dimorphotheca, Gypsophila, Lobelia, Phlox, Portulaca, Sweet alyssum, Verbena

Dwarf 8"-14"
Anemone, Arabis, Aster, Balsam, Begonia, Bergenia, Brachycome, Browallia, Candytuft, Chrysanthemum, Clarkia, Cornflower, Cyclamen, Geranium, Gloxinia, Hyacinth, Impatiens, Narcissus, Nemesia, Nicotiana, Ornithogalum, Petunia, Poppy, Primrose, Salvia, Snapdragon, Stock, Tulip, Vinca, Viola

Medium 16"-24"
Achillea, Agapanthus, Amaryllis, Anemone, Aster, Begonia, Caladium, Clarkia, Chrysanthemum, Cornflower, Dahlia, Dianthus, Freesia, Fuchsia, Gomphrena, Gypsophila, Impatiens, Iris, Lantana, Leucojum, Lupine, Lunaria, Maltese-cross, Marigold, Nicotiana, Nigella, Platycodon, Poppy, Ranunculus, Salvia, Schizanthus, Snapdragon, Tulip, Zinnia

Tall 30" or more
Aster, Calla lily, Campanula, Canna, Clematis (vine), Cleome, Cosmos, Dahlia, Delphinium, Digitalis, Euryops, Gladiolus, Hollyhocks, Iris, Lily, Lupine, Maltese-cross, Nierembergia, Salvia, Scabiosa, Statice, Sunflower, Sweet pea (vine), Thunbergia (vine), Zinnia

Red and Pink

Extra-dwarf up to 8"
Armeria, Begonia, Campanula, Coleus, Dianthus, Hyacinth, Kalanchoe, Nemesia, Nicotiana, Phlox, annual, Portulaca, Sweet alyssum, Tulip, Verbena, Vinca

Dwarf 8"-14"
Achimenes, Anemone, Arabis, Aster, Balsam, Begonia, Bergenia, Brachycome, Calceolaria, California poppy, Celosia, Chrysanthemum, Cineraria, Clarkia, Cuphea, Cyclamen, Dianthus, English daisy, Fuchsia, Gerbera, Gloxinia, Gomphrena, Impatiens, Kalanchoe, Nasturtium, Penstemon, Petunia, Primrose, Salvia, Saponaria, Snapdragon, Stock, Tulip, Vinca, Viola, Zinnia

Medium 16"-24"
Achillea, Allium, Amaryllis, Anemone, Aster, Begonia, Bergenia, Caladium, Chrysanthemum, Clarkia, Cornflower, Cosmos, Dahlia, Dianthus, English daisy, Erigeron, Flax, Freesia, Fuchsia, Gaillardia, Geranium, Geum, Gomphrena, Heuchera, Impatiens, Iris, Ixia, Lavatera, Linaria, Lupine, Maltese-cross, Marigold, Nicotiana, Nigella, Penstemon, Poppy, Ranunculus, Salvia, Schizanthus, Snapdragon, Tulip, Verbena, Veronica, Zinnia

Tall 30" or more
Amaranthus, Aster, Campanula, Canna, Clematis (vine), Cleome, Cockscomb celosia, Cosmos, Dahlia, Delphinium, Digitalis, Gladiolus, Hemerocallis, Hollyhock, Iris, Lily, Lupine, Maltese-cross, Poppy, Salpiglossis, Salvia, Scabiosa, Statice, Sweet pea (vine), Zinnia

Yellow

Extra-dwarf up to 8"
Achillea, Coleus, Crocus, Iris, Kalanchoe, Linum, Marigold, Nemesia, Portulaca, Sanvitalia, Tulip

Dwarf 8"-14"
Alyssum, Calceolaria, California poppy, Celosia, Chrysanthemum, Coreopsis, Gazania, Gerbera, Iris, Kalanchoe, Linum, Marigold, Narcissus, Nasturtium, Petunia, Primrose, Snapdragon, Tulip, Viola, Zinnia

Medium 16"-24"
Achillea, Calendula, Chrysanthemum, Coreopsis, Dahlia, Freesia, Gaillardia, Geum, Hypericum, Iris, Ixia, Layia, Linaria, Lupine, Marigold, Poppy, Iceland, Ranunculus, Snapdragon, Stock, Tulip, Zinnia

Tall 30" or more
Canna, Clematis (vine), Cockscomb celosia, Dahlia, Digitalis, Gladiolus, Hemerocallis, Hollyhock, Hypericum, Iris, Lily, Lupine, Marigold, Rudbeckia, Salpiglossis, Statice, Sunflower, Sweet Pea (vine), Thunbergia (vine)

Violet

Extra-dwarf up to 8"
Crocus, Gomphrena, Iris, Lobelia, Nierembergia, Portulaca, Scilla, Sweet alyssum, Tulip, Verbena

Dwarf 8"-14"
Achimenes, Anemone, Arabis, Aster, Balsam, Chrysanthemum, Gloxinia, Gomphrena, Impatiens, Iris, Penstemon, Petunia, Snapdragon, Tulip, Viola

Medium 16"-24"
Allium, Anemone, Aster, Chrysanthemum, Dahlia, Freesia, Fuchsia, Geranium, Gomphrena, Heliotrope, Impatiens, Iris, Lantana, Lavender, Linaria, Lunaria, Lupine, Nigella, Salvia, Snapdragon, Statice, Tulip, Verbena, Zinnia

Tall 30" or more
Aster, Clematis (vine), Cleome, Cosmos, Dahlia, Digitalis, Erigeron, Gladiolus, Hemerocallis, Hollyhock, Iris, Lily, Lupine, Ranunculus, Salpiglossis, Scabiosa, Schizanthus, Sweet pea (vine)

General Index

Picture Index